The
American Salad Book

By

Maximilian De Loup

The most complete, original and useful collection of Salad
Recipes ever brought together.

PREFACE.

N O apology is needed for the publication of a good Salad book at this time, and it is hoped that this volume will meet the wants of the American people,. in a practical, useful way. The recipes have been carefully collected from all parts of the world. After examination and test an enormous quantity have been rejected as being unfit or impossible for use on our tables. By far the best recipes are those that have originated in the United States and, almost without exception, they are alike in-expensive, elegant and heathful. Delicacy in food belongs to the higher civilization and those who have conquered the salad question are in a position to be envied. They can always add to the plainest dinner a desirable dish which will stimulate the fancy and give zest to the ap-petite of even the most fastidious.

CONTENTS.

"To Search the Secrets of a Salad."

America the Land of Salads.

TOO many Americans still follow the questionable fashion of thinking that foreign nations are ahead of us in salad making. France for a long time led in this as in many other delicate arts, but today she does not possess, or cannot import from distant countries, the great variety of delicious fruits and vegetables obtainable in so many sections of our own favored land. England is still barbaric in much of her salad serving and eating, and while the Teutonic salads are powerful, American palates cannot always relish them. Other nations are mostly imitative, as we have been in the past, while we are fast learning that originality and adaptation have given us the best the world affords.

Times change and we change with them. New things will doubtless continue to come into use, and in a measure, supersede the old, but when we reflect that fifty years ago tomatoes were scarce and called "Love Apples," being principally cultivated for ornament, we need not be surprised at the introduction and use of any of our native vegetable productions for salad materials.

We still eat too few green salads : our climate, varying with the changing seasons, demands an almost constant change of food. While the more highly seasoned compounds may be acceptable during the cold months, most of us feel a repugnance for them when hot weather comes, and long for something delicate and appetizing, yet cold.

As we cultivate a taste for wholesome green foods and learn to prefer them to heavy bulky materials, the supply will come in response to the demand, and the glory of the past that was once over other lands will come to us and successfully defy all rivals.

9

The Mixing of Salads.

"HEREIN the honor lies," fortunately for the less accomplished the simple salads are usually the most acceptable. No absolute rule can be laid down for the preparation of salads in a general way, except in special cases, although the most satisfactory plan is to keep them mild and not to allow one flavor to predominate but strive to have a delicate and appetizing blending of all. Most people have a favorite recipe for salad dressing but it will not do to be dogmatic in this respect, for it must be remembered that individual tastes widely differ and also that the taste of every person varies at different times, while there is always danger that a constant use of one dressing will soon vitiate or even render depraved the sense of taste. A person of strong constitution, accustomed to out of door life will enjoy a salad that would almost strangle a person of sedentary habits.

A good salad cannot be made of a lot of miscellaneous materials: the salad dresser must have good materials to achieve success, but if the materials are limited then the true skill of the artist is shown in concocting a dainty dish from what may be available.

Avoid giving all salads the same taste by flavoring them with some condiment one is perhaps over-fond of, but which is not so much appreciated by others. Variety is the main spice of salads as of life. While connoisseurs all agree that pure, fresh olive oil is the best for salads there are people who prefer the fat of smoked bacon and relish its flavor above all else. It is well, also, to remember that with abundant material at hand, we should know how to substitute one condiment for another, if necessary, and not go " salad-less " for want of one particular flavoring material. Salt is perhaps the one indispensable seasoning, and of all flavoring substances the onion is most valuable and enjoyable to all, even to those who would not willingly eat of the salad if they knew onion had been used. It will be understood, however, that for use in salads, the onions must be of mild flavor and their presence cunningly concealed, else the too pronounced use of any varieties of the onion family will cause an otherwise delicious and healthful salad to be politely declined by the over-fastidious guest.

Salads of all kinds should be gently handled. That is they should not be put into the desired shape by heavy pressure, but mixed by running the fork and spoon down the sides of the dish and then gently tossing the salad with an upward movement letting it mix as it falls back. In mixing a plain lettuce or other green salad it is well to put the oil on first and then carefully toss the leaves about until all are covered, in every part, with a thin coating of the oil. Then add the other ingredients and toss again. A small quantity of oil is sufficient when this method of thorough mixing is observed.

Decorating and Garnishing Salads.

THE pleasing art of table decorations, so happily possessed by American housekeepers, gives an opportunity for the salad artist to display taste and judgment, while originality is most commendable in the arrangement of this most ornamental of all dishes. The artistic eye is gladdened by the sight of a well arranged table and surely the sense of smell and sight should be pleased as well as that of taste, or the most delicious salad will fail of high success. Every dish should be in harmony with the table decorations and garnished in good taste without being unduly conspicuous.

The utmost cleanliness and freshness are indispensable. The least suggestion of insect ravages or decay of the foliage used in salads is abhorrent and a single faded leaf or the smallest bug will destroy the piquancy the salad would otherwise impart to the meal.

For some elaborate entertainments, when the salad bowl is placed on a platter or plaque, a pretty effect may be had by arranging blossoms of some fruit, apple, cherry or peach, around the bowl: the effect will be greatly heightened if the lower dish be of silver. Later in the season, blossoms of the rose, mignonette, sweet pea, honeysuckle or any attractive flower or leaf, may be used to advantage in garnishing the salad dishes. A thick bed of green mint is re-refreshing and harmonious while the foliage of carrots, parsley and sweet geraniums may also be used to advantage. A perfect salad, fresh and freshly mixed, is the most picturesque of all dishes, but a heavy garnish of boiled vegetables or eggs will detract from its light and delicate charm. A few of the inner heart leaves of lettuce are attractive laid lightly over a mayonnaise, and the blanched leaves of celery are appropriate when the stalks have been used in making the salad. Very small radishes, whole or cut into thin slices, are attractive scattered over green salads. With a little ingenuity and a sharp knife the radishes may be fashioned into the semblance of flowers and thus add to the attractiveness of the salad.

For winter decorations, with cold meats, the semblance of a marygold may be fashioned from a carrot, red and white roses from beets and turnips and other odd and attractive forms which will readily suggest themselves to the reader and which will add vastly to the attractiveness of not only the salad, but the entire table display.

A favorite Parisian top dressing for fish salads is composed of small crawfish: sometimes the meat is taken out and then replaced in the shells with a more piquant seasoning than that used in the body of the salad. Oysters, crabs and the coral of lobsters are also used in the same manner. The scarlet of the lobster acts as a trumpet call to our appetites. I would not, however, recommend the use of sea weeds in salads, for beyond rockweed used in a Rhode Island clam bake, Americans do not relish them. For fruit salads the pretty little strawberry tomato, or ground cherry, is useful as a garnish and has the merit of being a novelty to most of the present generation.

Salad Accompaniments.

THE best and most acceptable food to accompany salads is good bread and butter. True elegance of living consists not so much in what we have as in having the best of its kind, whatever it may be, and having it well served. For the sake of convenience, when a large company is to be served, thin slices of bread can be buttered and placed together like sandwiches. Have them of uniform size and thickness and packed close together on the dish, to prevent drying: if not to be eaten soon after being made cover with a damp napkin and keep in a cool place so that the butter will harden and the bread be firm. Spreading the butter on the loaf before cutting off the slice will fre· quently keep the particles of bread from crumbling. I do not approve of salad sandwiches for, if too dry, they are flavorless and if plenty of dressing is used, as it must be to keep them moist, they are inconvenient to handle. Just now the devotes of Fashion advocate fancy sandwiches and appetizers of every description. Care should be taken in serving these not to have the flavoring the same as that of the salad, but while different the contrast in taste should not be too marked.

Delicately flavored butter is easily made in the country where the materials can be had, and is very popular for use at afternoon teas and light entertainments. Those here given are among the best, most popular and novel when used as accompaniments to more heavy dishes.

Welsh Sandwiches are made by rubbing together one part of sweet butter and two parts of mild soft cheese flavored with mustard and herb vinegar : this mixture is placed between thin slices of bread. Much used with green salads.

Boston Brown Bread is especially appetizing used with lobster and other fish salads. Thin slices of the bread are cut and buttered the same as white bread. Sometimes leaves of lettuce are dipped in French dressing and placed between the slices of bread, forming lettuce sandwiches. If the bread is spread with cream or Neufchatel cheese they are called " Brunettes : " if made with water cress instead of lettuce the name " Cresslets " is given them. Sandwiches of this kind should not be made until just before eating. Graham or Brown bread made from whole wheat ground, is preferred by many to white bread. When used it should be buttered and served the same as white bread.

Nasturtium Sandwiches are delicate and delicious when made of white bread as described, with the petals of nasturtium flowers, or the very young leaves, placed between the thin buttered slices of bread. These sandwiches are used with any meat or fish salad. Decorate the plate with nasturtium blossoms to indicate what is contained in the sandwiches.

Herb Sandwiches. These are made of the usual thin slices of white bread buttered, with the addition of such herbs and seasoning as are fancied. Lettuce leaves are coated with mayonnaise or a little is spread on the bread before enclosing a leaf of lettuce between the two slices. Trim off any of the leaves that project around the edge of the bread. Pepper grass, water cress, etc., should be dipped in salted vinegar or French dressing before being used in this way. Strongly flavored herbs like mint should be minced and lightly sprinkled over the buttered bread before putting the slices together : a few whole leaves may be laid between the slices if preferred in this way. Peppermint sandwiches are usually well liked at five o'clock teas, and those of spearmint with mutton salads: summer savory or sweet marjoram sandwiches are used with any cold fowl or meat salads. This method of using herbs is generally considered preferable to putting them in the salad itself, thus enabling those who do not like the flavor to decline them without forgoing the salad. Parsley, sorrel, chervil, dandelion, chives, basil, thyme, balm, burnet, horseradish, curry powder, pickles and many other herbs in various forms may be used for sandwiches in a similar manner.

Cheese Sandwiches are more commonly served in Europe with or immediately after salads, than with us. To use Roquefort cheese, mix it with a little more than the same quantity of butter and spread on thin slices of bread, or on crackers. Minced parsley or chives may be added if desired. Fromage de Brie, and cheeses of a similar character, should be cut into thin strips and put between thin slices of buttered bread, adding herbs if desired. Neufchatel, cream cheese, cottage or pot cheese, can all be used by rubbing to a cream with good butter, a small quantity will suffice for the cream cheese, and seasoning with a little salt, paprika or cayenne pepper. Sometimes the yolks of hard boiled eggs are mixed with the cheese. Boston Brown bread, "sea foam" or any kind of thin delicate cracker may be used in place of white bread.

Flavored Butter can be made when fresh flowers are abundant: spread on delicate bread they are much appreciated served with fruit salads or five o'clock teas. Advantage is taken of the fact that freshly churned butter readily absorbs odors and flavors. The butter is cut into thin slices of good size and so arranged that most of the surface is exposed to the air: they are then put in large tight jars or boxes with a quantity of petals of rose, violet, honeysuckle. nasturtium or any other flower fancied, and kept tightly closed for several hours, or until the flowers are withered. With the more delicately flavored petals it may be necessary to repeat the operation to obtain the desired result. Spread the butter on thin slices of bread, placing two buttered sides together and cut into squares, triangles or fancy shapes. Arrange in a folded napkin in order to retain the odor. Ornament with the same variety of flower used in flavoring the butter.

Cheese Fingers for serving with salad, are made by sifting a cup of flour into a bowl, and then, with the fingers, rubbing a tablespoonful of butter into it, adding half a saltspoonful of salt, a little paprika or other mild pepper, and a smal¹ half teaspoonful of baking powder. Beat the yolk of one egg light and add to the mixture with four tablespoonfuls of grated cheese. Cold water should be added in sufficient quantities to make a soft dough that will roll well. Roll to about one-third of an inch in thickness and cut into strips half an inch wide and about four inches long. Grate a little cheese over them and bake in a biscuit pan to a delicate brown using an oven in moderate heat.

Cheese Balls to be served hot with salad, are made by mixing one cup of grated cheese, half a cup of fine bread crumbs, five drops of Worcestershire sauce and one egg well beaten. Mix well together and roll into small balls: place in a wire frying basket, and just before they are wanted, plunge the basket into boiling fat: allow them to remain until a light brown and serve at once.

Condiments.

—

THE use of condiments in salad dressings is most important and it seems unnecessary to say that they should be of the best quality obtainable, If of poor quality they will spoil the best efforts of the salad mixer. Find a good substitute, or change the dressing, but do not spoil a good dinner by using a poor salad.

Olive Oil is one of the most important condiments, nothing being equal to pure, fresh olive oil though many things are superior to oil of poor or indifferent quality. As the production of olives increases in this country it will be easier to get the oil pure and fresh. Good oil may be obtained in any of our large cities although the finest product is still a luxury. Keep the bottled oil tightly corked in a cool dark place of even temperature.

Pepper is one of the most variable of all seasonings for not only does it lose strength rapidly when exposed to the air, but fresh pepper varies greatly which makes its use largely a matter of good judgment, and renders it difficult to give exact quantities to be used in any recipe. An air tight box is better to keep pepper in than the bottles with perforated tops such as are commonly used. The best way to prepare black pepper for salads is to buy the whole kernel and, with a small hand mill, grind what little is used each time: we are thus reasonably sure of its strength and purity. Somewhat coarse pepper is preferable to the very fine in salad making. Coarse pepper is sometimes called "mignonette" pepper the same name being applied to the whole white pepper. Black and white pepper are from the same

18

plant, the black being the outside of the .berry and the white the inside, after the black husk has been removed. Different names are given to the same variety of pepper according to the country in which it is grown. Red pepper is of many kinds but may be divided into simply mild and strong although of all degrees of intensity. It has always been justly considered healthful, mildly stimulating and an aid to digestion. Cayenne is the name usually given to the more pungent kinds although by no means do all of them come from Cayenne. A small quantity of Cayenne pepper is the best of all the pungent condiments for mayonnaise dressing. Paprika is a Hungarian name given to mild red pepper and is fast coming into general use as it may be used for general flavoring purposes without obtaining the pungency which always goes with Cayenne pepper and which, to many people, is most objectionable.

Salt is too well known to need description. For use in salads it should be fine and dry and is best kept in a warm dry closet.

Mustard, as we know it in seasoning, is the flour of black and white mustard seeds ground together. It varies greatly in strength and quality: if poor and musty a small quantity will suffice to spoil a salad. Mustard is usually mixed with warm water: hot water will make it flat. French mustard is the same flour of mustard seeds mixed with Tarragon vinegar and oil in small quantities and is, practically, the same as German mustard. Sugar and spices are often added in the manufacture of prepared mustards. The mustard used for salads in Europe is frequently mixed with Maderia, sherry and other wines but this is a matter of individual taste in all cases. The young leaves of the mustard plant are an addition to any green salad.

Vinegar is made from many different substances and all are good if fermentation is obtained by the natural process

and not by the use of chemicals. Good vinegar is not difficult to procure but there is much of it sold which is so
adulterated and the taste and odor so pronounced it will
spoil any salad. White wine vinegar being colorless, or
nearly so, is considered the best for salads but the red vinegars are always acceptable while orange vinegar is liked
where it is known.

Flavored Vinegars are good and convenient to use when
we cannot get green herbs. The flavoring of vinegar with
herbs is a simple process ordinarily nothing being required
but to put the clean herbs in a bottle, cover them with vinegar and then heat by putting the bottles in a kettle of cold
water and boiling, taking the bottles out as soon as the
water boils. The vinegar is sometimes boiled and poured
hot over the herbs in the bottle: let the bottle stand until
cool and then cork. If the flavor is too strong the vinegar
may be poured off and diluted. All flavored vinegars are
better if allowed to remain in the tightly corked bottles for
ten days or two weeks before using Tarragon vinegar is
the best known of the flavored vinegars and is deservedly
popular. Chervil vinegar is especially desirable for use in
fish sauces and salads. Mint in its various varieties can be
used. Spearmint is excellent in mutton salads and in mint
sauce when the fresh mint cannot be obtained. Onions,
celery leaves or stalks, sweet Basil, chives, Sweet Cicely,
small and strong peppers, shallots, summer savory, sweet
marjoram, nasturtiums and other herbs and plants can be
used for flavoring vinegars as can also celery seeds and
Cayenne. Cucumber vinegar is made by slicing ten large
cucumbers in a quart of vinegar with two onions, two shallots and salt and pepper to suit the taste. Let the mixture
stand for five days, boil, strain, cool and bottle tightly.

Serving Salads.

S OME lovers of salads consider it a social offense to serve
one improperly. Fortunately for the many housekeepers, both public and private, who cater to the tastes of
the great American public, our lawmakers have not yet
taken that view of it. The good natured American people
go on eating what is set before them or mildly decline it
without protest, although no nation of people is more appre-
ciative of the best when they can get it. Attention to the
minor morals of cookery will do far more to bring "good
will among men" than more pretentious efforts.

To learn to serve a salad is a most important qualifica-
tion for one who would "master the art of entertaining."
An exception to the rule, that new dishes should not be
served for company, is often made with salads, for without
a new salad a dinner party does not attain the height of
success.

It is said as much judgment and skill are required to
serve a dinner correctly as to manage a railroad: and I be-
lieve more good men could be found for the latter occupa-
tion than could meet criticism successfully, with the con-
coction and serving of dinners.

Environment is much. A rough salad with plenty of
vinegar and no oil will be consumed with a greater zest by
hungry men in camp than would be possible to obtain in a
well appointed dining room.

To become a proficient salad mixer do not attempt too
much at first: practice on plain salads and dressings before
elaborating them: study the tastes of your guests as well as
the mixing of condiments.

Any salad, and most of all a plain one, should not be prepared until just before it is to be eaten. Some of the most elaborate ones have the fish or meat marinated (See caption Marinade under "Salad Dressings and Sauces,") before being put together, but even with these the final mixing should be done just before eating. It is not in good taste to prepare a salad at the table excepting to mix with the dressing, for while the process interests many it annoys more. If the final mixing is done by a servant it had better be done at a side table.

The rich and elaborate salads should be served by themselves, accompanied by good bread and butter, or sandwiches that harmonize in flavor or accentuate that of the salad. When the salad itself is to accompany a dish of meat it should be simple in character and be served on small cold plates. We enjoy a plain lettuce or celery salad with broiled or roast chicken according to the season. With wild ducks, celery and fried hominy. With the Christmas boars' head, or roast pig in winter, a salad of blanched dandelion or endive, even if quite bitter, is most relished. An acid salad made with sour fruits or with a good proportion of fresh lime or lemon juice, is always acceptable with water fowl. With salmon and other fish, cucumbers are always proper. When many guests, especially strangers, are to be served it is best to have two or more kinds of salad dressing and let each one help themselves to that which they like best.

A well made salad will not produce dyspepsia if eaten in moderation, but like everything else it should be eaten slowly.

What to drink with salads has been the subject of much dispute among connoisseurs. I consider the best advice is to drink as little as possible of anything while eating. When wines are served, either red or white wine is best with dinner or luncheon salads. Under no circumstances serve a sweet wine with fruit salads.

Many people enjoy cheese served with green salads.

Bread and butter, cream cheese and cresses will remind many city readers of delightful country retreats. Cheese straws and other preparations of cheeses and pastry can accompany a salad as well.

"It is recommended very strongly that the salad nicely arranged in a bowl, and the ice cold sauce in its boat should be presented separately and handed round together." This plan has the merit of economy in saving the waste which would result if the mixing was previously done and the salad was not all used.

Let those who enjoy a "retiring dish" before going to bed, and who think they sleep better for eating at that time, try a salad of lettuce, celery or onions. They are all soporific in their effects besides being easy of digestion. Celery is soothing to the nerves and the medicinal qualities of the onion family are manifold while the offensive odor is less prominent at night than during the day.

Salad Dressings and Sauces.

MUCH has been written by salad masters on the importance of giving the utmost care and attention to the dressing of salads, for on this depends the success of the whole. The kind of dressings are numerous, almost innumerable, but the really good ones are indeed few. The French or plain dressing and the mayonnaise are in almost universal use throughout the civilized world and, with slight variations, are more generally approved than any other kind. Indeed, were they always to be had, directions for others would be nearly superfluous, but often good materials cannot be obtained and although good judges insist upon a liberal quantity of oil being used there are many people who will eat nothing into which olive oil enters. It is said that a true salad artist never measures anything so nicely does he adapt the seasoning to the conditions and to the requirements of his guests. This is all very well where we have knowledge and experience, but with new things and new people a guide is necessary. In all directions given in this book, such quantities and proportions are used as experience has shown meet the average taste: however, nothing is absolute for the strength of the several condiments vary greatly, and, of course, a salad of salty materials will require less of that condiment in the dressing, and one of peppergrass, or other strong herbs, less pepper.

Much has been written about mayonnaise and we are told that properly it includes the whole preparation, meat, herbs and dressing, but the term as used in the United States has been so long and universally applied to dressing alone that it would be misleading to attempt a change. Still, it should

be understood, when other things than egg, oil, vinegar or
lemon juice, salt, pepper and mustard are added it is not a
mayonnaise dressing but should be given another name. A
perfect mayonnaise is a triumph of art: with good materials
it is easily made but when the materials are poor the dressing is, to put it mildly, indifferent.

The process of dropping oil from a bottle, as we get it in
this country, may be facilitated by cutting two grooves in
the cork on opposite sides, one for the oil to run out of
and the other to admit the air.

It is held by many salad makers that a small quantity of
sugar, often little more than a " pinch, " should be added to
all salad dressings for the purpose of bringing to gether the
other seasonings in more perfect affinity. It will do no
harm if enough is not put in to give the dressing a sweet
taste, but the moment this occurs the salad is spoiled, unless, of course, a sweet salad is wanted.

" **Chapon,** " for Green Salads. Cut from a loaf of bread
a thin crust about one inch by two, sprinkle it with salt
and rub with a clove of garlic crushed: toss the bread into
the bottom of the salad bowl, before the salad is put in,
and let remain in the salad during the process of mixing:
remove before serving the salad.

MAYONNAISE DRESSINGS.

Have all the materials ready, clean and cold, when
about to begin. Do the mixing in a cool place and
if the weather is hot set the bowl on ice before or
during the mixing. A shallow bowl or soup plate is most
convenient for beating. Use a silver or wooden fork or
smooth wooden spoon. Have the yolks of two fresh raw
eggs and two hard boiled ones in a cool bowl, drop on a
little oil and rub to a cream: then add a teaspoonful of
made English mustard (made by mixing ground mustard
with warm water) two teaspoonfuls of dry fine salt and a

sprinkle of Cayenne pepper: then drop in oil, drop by drop, stirring and beating hard all the time until the mixture is thick and solid enough to keep its shape and have a glassy look. It will require from eight tablespoonfuls to half a pint of oil, according to size of eggs and quality of materials. Thin the mixture by dropping in vinegar until the dressing is of proper consistency: about two tablespoonfuls of vinegar will be required. A few drops of lemon juice may be added but avoid using too much or it will give the dressing an acidity very unpleasant. Keep the dressing in a cold place until wanted. Just before using, the whites of the raw eggs are usually beaten to a stiff froth and then beaten into the dressing. If, when partly made, it "breaks" or curdles, put in a cool place and when ready begin over again with more egg and instead of using oil drop the curdled dressing into the bowl until it is used. This dressing is always acceptable for any of the numerous green, meat or fish salads where mayonnaise is wanted, but is subject to countless variations according to taste or fancy. When more eggs are used less oil is required, and vice versa. If a very mild dressing should be wanted, omit the mustard and pepper. This is the kind usually preferred for fresh fruit salads. For fruit salads a spoonful of fine sugar can be substituted for the mustard. For sweet fruit it can be made more acid and for acid fruit less so. Cream, if thick and fresh, can sometimes be used to advantage with less oil, especially for fruit and fresh vegetables. Keep in a separate dish and do not mix with other things until just before eating. The process of mixing should take from ten to fifteen minutes. When wanted to coat meats or fish use aspic jelly in place of raw eggs, warming it sufficient to melt and then putting the coated dish in an ice chest. This is sometimes called a "jelly mayonnaise."

White Mayonnaise. This is made by using less egg yolk and more lemon juice in place of vinegar, the acid of the lemon always tending to whiten the eggs. The addition of the beaten white of egg and cream also tend to make it white. If a golden yellow color is wished all these ingredients should be omitted.

Green Mayonnaise is prepared by using a little spinach juice in plain mayonnaise, or the juice of any fresh salad herbs, tarragon, burnet, or chives may be used if desired. The prepared colorings that may be bought of grocers are cheap and convenient and should not be harmful. Very soft mashed green peas are used to give color and consistency when the dressing is used to cover fish.

Red Mayonnaise is made by adding some of the prepared coloring, cooked beet juice or highly colored fruit juice to plain mayonnaise. For fish salads, pound the coral of lobster, mix with a little oil and when smooth add to the mayonnaise.

Horseradish Mayonnaise is made by adding about three tablespoonfuls of fresh grated horseradish to the given amount of plain mayonnaise, or, if prepared horseradish is used, take the same amount and use the vinegar in which it is packed instead of plain vinegar. This is a good relish on cold beef and fish salads.

English Salad Sauce, so called, is mayonnaise with eggs in the proportion of two hard boiled to one raw yolk, and about two-thirds as much thick sweet cream as oil, the whole being well beaten together for twenty minutes or more and then cooled in the ice chest.

Mayonnaise Tartare is simply the addition of a little chopped onions or of onion juice, chopped cucumber pickles or capers and parsley, chives, chopped olives or any green herb the flavor of which is desired.

MISCELLANEOUS SAUCES.

The following sauces are, without exception, easily made

and of such variety that it is possible to have a desirable change with nearly every salad made. The variety will be most welcome to those whose sole dependence has been the French and Mayonnaise dressings.

Remoulade Sauce is made the same as mayonnaise sauce without the raw eggs, the yolks of hard boiled eggs alone being used. This is designed for the convenience of those to whom raw eggs are objectionable.

Viniagrette Sauce. Mix together one tablespoonful of of vinegar, three of oil, one teaspoonful each of chopped parsley, capers and scraped or grated onion. Season with one saltspoonful of salt and pepper or a few drops of tobasco sauce.

Viniagrette Sauce with Egg. Mash the yolk of a hard boiled egg with three tablespoonfuls of oil, two of vinegar, a finely chopped shallot, one teaspoonful of chopped chives or half a teaspoonful of onion juice, as preferred, a salt-spoonful of salt and half as much pepper, Cayenne pepper preferred.

Bacon Sauce. Made by frying thin slices of smoked bacon or ham fat and after straining, add one-third vinegar to two-thirds bacon oil. It may be thickened by adding a little flour mixed with cold water and then cooking. This is greatly relished on green salads, by many people, and is often available in camp or other places where olive oil is not to be had.

Boiled Salad Dressing. This is best made with a double boiler, or *bain marie* or in a small kettle in a larger one of boiling water. The yolks and whites of three eggs are beaten separately and stirred in the boiler with one cup of cream or rich milk, one-quarter teacup of vinegar, one teaspoonful each of mustard and pepper. Cook slowly and when thick stir in two teaspoonfuls of salt. If too thick, thin with more cream, melted butter or oil. Butter or oil can be used instead of cream using more milk to keep it from being too hard. Add a good teaspoonful of sugar if it is relished. Stir constantly when boiling and when cooling to make it smooth.

Boiled Salad Dressing No. 2. Yolks of eight eggs, one cup of cream, (if milk is used put in a little butter) one pint of vinegar, one teaspoonful of sugar. Put in a double boiler or bowl in boiling water and cook to a cream but not until it is solid. Take from the fire and add one tablespoonful of salt, one of black pepper and one of mustard, well mixed and rubbed together with oil until all the lumps are dissolved. More oil may be added to thin the dressing if the taste is desired.

Sour Cream Salad Dressing. To a cupful of thick cream, sour but not too old, add a teaspoonful of salt, the juice of half a lemon, two teaspoonfuls of vinegar, a good sprinkling of Cayenne, or if a mild pepper is preferred use paprika in larger quantities, and a teaspoonful of sugar. Beat all together thoroughly. This is relished on salads of cold boiled vegetables and on tomatoes.

Albert Dressing. Four tablespoonfuls of oil are well mixed with one each of wine and vinegar. A teaspoonful of salt and a little paprika or other mild red pepper is added.

Tomato Dressing. Put in a frying pan two tablespoonfuls of butter, an onion of medium size sliced thin, and a small green pepper of the strong variety: a little Cayenne may be used if the green pepper is not available. Fry until highly colored, add about two cupfuls of tomatoes, cook and stir until the tomatoes are reduced to a pulp. Strain the mixture, return to the frying pan and thicken with an even teaspoonful of flour stirred in cold water. Let it cook slowly for nearly half an hour, seasoning with salt and a little clove or any other spice preferred. If too thick, thin

with a little oil or hot water. To be eaten on any green
salad with cold meats.

Sardine Dressing. Take two sardines free from bones
and skin, mash fine with one raw egg, one tablespoonful of
oil, two of vinegar, one teaspoonful of made mustard, one of
salt and one-quarter teaspoonful of pepper. Stir well together and add a small quantity of chopped parsley. Serve
with fish salads or meat.

East Indian Salad Dressing. The yolks of two hard
boiled eggs rubbed smooth with eight tablespoonfuls of oil,
a teaspoonful of curry powder and two tablespoonfuls of
Tarragon vinegar.

Salmi Sauce. Take half a carrot of medium size and
cut into small pieces: half an onion, two bay leaves, a
sprig of thyme and six whole pepper corns. Put these into
a sauce pan with an ounce of butter and cook briskly for
about five minutes or until all are of a golden yellow color.
Chop the trimmings from the bird used and add to contents
of the sauce pan, together with half a wineglassful of sherry,
half a cupful of mushroom liquor, the juice of one lemon, a
saltspoonful of salt, half as much pepper and a little nutmeg. Let all cook together for twenty minutes and then
strain for use.

Almond Salad Dressing. For ripe peaches, sliced bananas, pears, fresh figs or any kind of ripe fruit the following dressing will be found most excellent.

To every dozen sweet almonds allow four bitter ones.
Blanch and remove the brown skins, then soak them in cold
water for two hours and pound in a marble or a porcelain
lined mortar, adding a little salt, a slight sprinkling of Cayenne pepper and a little lemon juice. When all are ground
fine, thin with sherry wine to the consistency of cream.
Just before using cold fresh cream can be stirred into it. If

the fresh cream makes it too rich it may be omitted without detriment.

Lemon Dressing. This is a most healthful and refreshing dressing to serve on lettuce or any green salad, and is frequently more relished by children and convalescents than any other dressing. Squeeze the juice from a lemon and add as much cold water as juice, half a saltspoonful of salt and a teaspoonful of fine sugar.

Hollandaise Sauce. Especially good to use with fish salads when good oil is difficult to obtain. Rub half a cup of butter to a cream and add, slowly, the yolks of two eggs. Also add a saltspoonful of salt, a sprinkle of Cayenne pepper and the juice of one lemon. Pour in half a cupful of boiling water and stand the bowl in a pan of boiling water or in the top of a tea kettle and stir until thick as cream.

Bernaise Sauce. Beat the yolks of four eggs and add four tablespoonfuls of oil, one of hot water and one of vinegar, Tarragon or plain: one teaspoonful of salt and a sprinkling of Cayenne pepper. Boil in a double boiler or on a kettle until thick, adding the vinegar last. It should be like firm mayonnaise. By adding chopped pickles, capers, or olives with a few drops of Tobasco sauce a good sauce Tartare can be made.

Mexican Salad Dressing. Crush fine in a stone or porcelain lined mortar a clove of garlic the size of a small pea and two small strong green peppers that have been boiled or roasted: add also three tomatoes of medium size that have been boiled and peeled. Grind all together thoroughly and pour over lettuce or cold boiled potatoes that have been dressed with salt, oil and vinegar.

Italian Salad Dressing. Rub an anchovy quite smooth with a tablespoonful of oil and a teaspoonful of made mustard. Add three or four more tablespoonfuls of oil, one of garlic vinegar, and one of common vinegar. Stir until creamy and serve in a dish separate from the salad.

Salad Dressing with Cheese. Rub four tablespoonfuls of oil into the yolks of two hard boiled eggs, then add a teaspoonful of grated Parmesan cheese, one of made mustard, one of Tarragon vinegar and a tablespoonful of cider vinegar. A spoonful of mushroom, walnut or other catsup can be added if the flavor is desired.

Ravigote Butter. Chop very fine, or pound in a mortar, equal parts of Tarragon, parsley and chervil seasoned with a sprinkle of salt and pepper. Rub one tablespoonful of these mixed herbs into one-quarter pound of fresh butter and then put on ice to set. When ready to use cut with slightly warmed cutter into pretty shapes for garnishing.

Ravigote Sauce. Put the yolks of two raw eggs and one ounce of butter into a small sauce pan or *bain marie* and place over the fire where it is not too hot and stir until it begins to thicken: add an ounce more of butter and stir again until it makes a cream. Then add pounded herbs, of chives use half a teaspoonful or a teaspoonful each of burnet, chervil, tarragon, parsley and others to suit the taste. Celery, bay leaves, capers, mustard, cresses and anchovies are sometimes added. It is made without cooking by using the yolk of one raw egg, and oil instead of butter: beat to a cream and add finely minced or powdered herbs.

Cucumber Jelly. Peel and cut off the green ends of four large or five small cucumbers, cut into slices and stew in a quart of water with a small slice of onion, a little pepper and a small teaspoonful of salt. When the cucumbers become soft, stir in half a box of gelatine that has been previously soaked in a cupful of water. Stir until the gelatine is dissolved and then strain through a fine sieve or strainer and put in moulds to harden. This is good with any fish salad, especially salmon. The fish can be flaked, put in the mould and hardened with the jelly. If served by itself sliced cucumbers are good in it. It can be moulded in small egg cups or in individual moulds as preferred. This jelly is never more attractive than when surrounding a mound of pink salmon on a bed of fresh lettuce, the jelly broken and sparkling. French dressing should be used with it. Serve as cold as possible.

Tomato Jelly. One quart of tomatoes, one small onion sliced, a few sprigs of parsley, three or four cloves, salt and a sprinkling of Cayenne, or a small hot pepper from the garden, are used in making this jelly. Stew the mixture until the tomatoes are soft, strain and add half a box of gelatine that has been soaked in a cup of water. There should be a little more than a pint of the liquid. Use as a garnish for meat or green salads. A large mould of the jelly on a bed of lettuce surrounded by mayonnaise is very attractive. Individual moulds on separate plates are convenient to serve with a large company. Use mayonnaise dressing with this jelly.

Marinade. When meat or fish is dry and tasteless it is improved by putting in a marinade or sauce to stand for a time, one or two hours usually being sufficient. A plain marinade is made by using one part oil to three parts vinegar, with pepper and salt to taste. Other flavors, sweet herbs, spices, etc., can be given by bruising in a little oil and letting them stand before mixing with the rest. The use of marinade is usually carried to excess, the quantity of vinegar poured on destroying all other flavors. Use only enough to season the meat and only what will be absorbed by the meat.

Cutting Meats for Salads. Meat of all kinds for use in salads should be cut into uniform small slices or cubes as far as possible. If cut into pieces do not have them too small: a half inch is about right. If smaller, or if chopped,

it suggest hash, becomes wet and soggy with the dressing
and is always unpleasant to the taste.   When meat or fish
of different kinds are put in the same salad, however, they
need not be cut in equal sizes.

French or Plain Salad Dressing.   Take three tablespoonfuls of sweet oil, one saltspoonful of salt, one-half saltspoonful of pepper, and one-quarter of a teaspoonful of onion
juice.   Mix well and quickly and throw over the salad.
This is the most popular of all salad dressings and the proportions are those generally approved, but are, of course,
subject to many variations some of which follow.

Variations.   When onion flavor is objectionable it can be
omitted but it gives a zest no other condiment affords.   It
should be used only in small quantities, never enough in a
dressing to overpower the other seasonings.   Those who are
exceedingly fond of it should have onion salads, than which
none are more healthful and invigorating.   When introduced
judiciously into a salad, onions are usually relished even by
the most strenuous objectors to the vegetable who will not
notice it in the salad when perfectly blended with the other
ingredients and without strong odor.   A few drops of juice,
squeezed out with a porcelain lined lemon squeezer and
mixed with the oil is the preferred way of introducing it,
but if the onion juice cannot be readily used, scrape a little
of the raw onion and mix with a part of the oil, let it stand
for fifteen minutes or longer then press the oil out and mix
with the dressing.

When garlic is used, rub a crushed clove of it on the bottom of the bowl in which the dressing is mixed, or, if mixed
in the French manner by working the oil over the lettuce
first, rub the garlic on a small piece of stale bread, called
in France the " chapon," and toss it about in the bowl with
the salad, rubbing some salt over it after the garlic is used.

When the slight flavor of strong herbs is relished in a
salad, a small quantity of them can be crushed in a stone

or porcelain mortar and then macerated or soaked in a little oil, which may be pressed out with a thin spoon and added to the dressing. Summer savory or thyme can thus be used in a plain salad to accompany roasted or broiled poultry. Sweet marjoram or sage is used with green geese or ducks, mint with lamb or venison and sweet basil with fish or clams. Orange flowers, or the tender buds and leaves, may be used. Basil, burnet, caraway, balm, chervil or any other herbs may be used in place of those mentioned, taste being the guide in all cases.

English Salad Dressing is made by the addition of a teaspoonful of made mustard to the given quantity of French dressing.

ERRATUM.

French or Plain Salad Dressing, Page 34. Read as follows. " Take three tablespoonfuls of sweet oil, *one of vinegar*, one saltspoonful of salt etc., etc.

Fish Salads.

ALMOST any kind of cold cooked fish can be acceptably served as a salad, that which is boiled being generally preferred. If a small quantity of vinegar is added to the water in which the fish is boiled, it will make the flesh firm yet tender.

Fish salads require the addition of fresh acids, lemon juice being the most grateful addition to the fish that is at all insipid as are some of the fresh water kinds. Stewed gooseberries are much liked as a dressing or accompaniment by many and may be properly used with any cooked fish. Chervil vinegar or a few leaves of fresh chervil impart a delightful relish. Fennel is also good for the same purpose.

Remove most carefully all scales, bones or skin that may remain on the fish before mixing a salad, but do not divide the flesh in too small pieces. In the case of a large fish the salad looks best and is most appetizing when the natural "flakes" are simply separated, without being broken, and lightly mixed in the salad.

Cucumber salad is the best accompaniment to fresh salmon, with plain dressing : or cucumber jelly may be used by way of variety. A boiled fish served whole as a salad is best for suppers or collations, but in warm weather it makes a good fish course for dinner when more or less elaborately decorated.

Cold chicory salad is delightful with deviled crabs or lobsters.

Herring Salad. Take fresh herring of large size and boil until tender. Remove the skin and bones and cut the fish diagonally in halves. Pour over it a dressing made as follows. For three pounds of fish take one pint of vinegar, two teaspoonfuls of whole pepper, two of allspice and three whole cloves. Mix the vinegar, allspice, cloves and two bay leaves together and heat slowly, but do not boil, for twenty minutes. When entirely cold mix with the salad. Between each layer of fish lay two bay leaves and two or three slices of red onion. Salt to taste. Garnish with small pickles and slices of red beets. Small thin slices of buttered brown bread should be served with this salad.

English Herring Salad. Soak four large, or six medium sized salted herring in cold water to draw out the salt, then pick the meat from the bones, divide into small pieces, and mix with an equal quantity of cold meat using veal, mutton or beef as preferred: then add three hard boiled eggs, two large boiled potatoes and two apples all cut into small pieces. Cucumbers and beets may also be added if desired. Stir together a quarter of a teacupful of rich cream, half as much vinegar and a little sugar and pepper and mix with the other things. Place the mixture in the centre of a platter and surround with a sauce of cream, vinegar, mustard and sugar, or with oil, vinegar and pepper. Chop a hard boiled egg and sprinkle the particles over the salad.

Herring Salad with Potatoes. Wash four salt herring and soak in milk for several hours, then drain, remove the fillets from the sides and cut into small pieces. Cut eight ounces of cold boiled potatoes, four ounces of tart apples, four ounces of pickled beets, (the roots) and four ounces of pickled cucumbers into pieces about a quarter of an inch square. Then mince very fine half a pound of roast veal and mix with the other things in a salad bowl, seasoning with salt and vinegar, pepper, mustard and chopped chives. Sprinkle chopped parsley over the top and decorate with anchovies, pickles and hard boiled eggs. Use a little more dressing or hot water if not sufficiently moist.

Dutch Herring Salad. This is said to be the true Hol-

land herring salad but by the addition of other fruits and
vegetables it becomes an Italian or a Russian salad.

Four large, or five small Holland herring are soaked in
milk or water three hours, and then cut into small square
pieces after all the skin and bones are carefully picked out.
Cut two quarts of hot boiled potatoes into slices, pour over
them enough Rhine wine to moisten them and keep in a close
covered dish until cold. Chop the yolks of four hard boiled
eggs and mix with the potatoes and fish. Season with
coarse black pepper freshly ground. If the fish are with
roe, soak in vinegar or Rhine wine a few minutes, then
separate the roe and sprinkle them over the salad. If milt-
herring, pound the milt to a paste, thin with wine or vinegar and pour over the rest.

Fresh Herring Salad. Clean and remove the heads from
two fresh herring, split in two and sprinkle with salt and
lemon juice, and let them stand for three hours. Dry and
broil, rubbing a little butter over them Remove bones,
skin, etc., and divide into small pieces. Pick the leaves
from a small handful of cress and put in a salad bowl with
the herring, adding two or three cold potatoes cut into
slices. Pour over all a plain salad dressing, sprinkle with
capers, mix and serve.

Smoked Herring Salad. Carefully separate the meat
from two good sized American smoked herring and divide
into small pieces. Mix in a salad bowl with one head of
lettuce and a plain dressing with some hard boiled eggs.
If preferred mix with a remoulade sauce.

Herring Salad, Italian Style. The meat of two salt herring is soaked in milk or water three hours and then cut
up fine. To half a pound of roast veal and a quarter of a
pound of Bologna sausage add three tart apples, three cold
boiled potatoes, sliced, and four or five small pickled beets
with a small quantity of some other desired pickle, minced

fine. Make a dressing of the milt of herring rubbed to a paste, with six tablespoonfuls of sweet oil: add half a teaspoonful of white or black pepper, a teaspoonful of French or German mustard, three of vinegar (tarragon.) Mix thoroughly and pour over the salad. This salad is improved, in the estimation of many people, by standing in a cold place for two hours before serving.

Frog Salad. This is one of the most delicate and delicious of all salads. Clean and skin the frogs and soak in salted water about an hour. If large frogs can be had, the greater part of the body can be used, but of the small frogs, called in the market Canadian frogs, the legs only are worth troubling with. Boil slowly until quite tender: drain off the water, cover with milk and let this come to a boil being careful that the milk does not burn. Drain again and cool, separate the meat from the bones and salt a little if too fresh. Then mix in a salad bowl with about the same quantity of young lettuce, or if lettuce is not obtainable celery may be used. A few leaves of water cress may be added, or a little minced parsley, or sweet basil but do not add enough strong herbs or seasoning to destroy the delicacy of the meat. Serve with a mild mayonnaise or French dressing. Hard boiled eggs for garnishing will increase the quantity of a small salad, or cray-fish may be used for this purpose where they are obtainable.

Mackerel Salad No. 1. This is made the same a Herring Salad using mackerel instead of herring.

Mackerel Salad No. 2. Boil fresh mackerel slowly for about twenty-five minutes or half an hour, drain, cool and pick all the good meat from the bones, skin and separate it into small pieces but do not chop or hash it. Put it in a salad bowl with heart leaves of lettuce, one large head or two small ones to each fish. Salt the water the fish was boiled in, or sprinkle a little fine salt over the prepared fish.

Serve with remoulade sauce or French dressing. Tiny clams, hard boiled eggs, spiced mussels, or shrimp are good for garnishing.

Mackerel Salad No. 3. Salt or pickled mackerel make a salad very relishing in early spring when other materials are scarce. Boil the fish and pick over carefully: mix cold boiled potatoes and fresh cress with the fish in the proportion of two-thirds of the fish to one-third of both vegetables, and serve with French dressing. Celery and potatoes are also good with this fish.

Salad of Shad Roe. Separate the grains of a shad roe boiled in salted water, by washing in vinegar. Place in a salad bowl with the leaves of one head of lettuce and one pint of tomatoes peeled and cut small. Dress with three tablespoonfuls of oil, and two of lemon juice with salt and Cayenne pepper or tobasco sauce to taste. The large roe of any fish is excellent treated in the same manner. Another way is to boil the roe in salted water with a sliced onion, a bay leaf or any herb fancied, for about twenty-five minutes. Then remove and drop into iced water. When perfectly cold, drain and cut into small slices. Sprinkle with salt, pepper and a little lemon juice and put on ice until wanted. When ready to serve mix with leaves of water cress and place on lettuce. Serve with boiled, mayonnaise or French dressing.

Salmon Salad (American.) Cold boiled salmon is usually served whole in this country covered with firm mayonnaise often elaborately colored and ornamented. Many caterers pride themselves on their skill in serving it. Being a fish that stands freezing and transportation on ice with less loss of flavor than most kinds, it is available in most parts of the country.

Boil the fish in salted water in which half a cup of good vinegar has been poured, if the fish is a large one: a less quantity of vinegar will do for a small fish. Boil for half an hour if a small fish, longer if large, allowing ten to twelve minutes for each pound of fish after boiling begins: better boil too long than to have the fish under-done. A bunch of sweet herbs sometimes called a "bouquet" can be boiled with the fish, the bouquet being composed of thyme, celery leaves, parsley, bay leaves, basil, etc. Small sliced onions and cloves will give the herbs additional flavor and be relished by many, but care should be taken not to season the fish so highly as to destroy the natural flavor and delicacy so pronounced in a good fish. A piece of clean muslin or mosquito netting wrapped around the fish and tied will prevent its boiling to pieces. If wanted whole, place on a long platter, or board, covered with a napkin, after removing the fins, skin and small bones. Place on ice and when cold cover with a stiff mayonnaise colored and decorated as may be fancied. If broken or part of a fish, divide into flakes or small pieces, do not mince, and arrange in a small salad bowl with good lettuce and serve with mayonnaise dressing. Decorate by placing a few of the pinkest and best formed flakes on top. When canned salmon has to be served this method of preparation is the best. Serve a plain dressing if preferred. Celery is sometimes used instead of lettuce but is not so good. A few water cresses are good to serve with fresh salmon.

Salmon Salad (English.) After being carefully cleaned and scalded, boil the fish in a stew pan with thin slices of onions, carrots and mushrooms, a bunch of sweet herbs, salt, pepper, spice and a glass of white wine. Cut the fish into slices as thin as a silver half dollar and set them around the dish. Garnish with hearts of lettuce, hard boiled eggs, slices of boiled carrots, gherkins, anchovies and capers. Make a cold ravigote sauce and pour over the whole.

Broiled Salmon Salad is made by broiling the fish in steaks instead of boiling: in this way it takes less time to prepare the fish and is more convenient. Broil the fish and when well done remove the bones and skin, break the fish into flakes and put in a dish with salt, pepper, vinegar or lime juice sprinkled over it, using only a very little oil as the fish is naturally rich and oily. Let it stand about an hour and then dress in a salad bowl with lettuce and mayonnaise dressing. If lettuce is not to be had, cold boiled potatoes may be used instead, and a few cresses will be a welcome addition. Hard boiled eggs and chopped cucumber pickles or capers are relished with this salad.

Salmon and Cucumbers make a good salad served with French dressing both to be fresh and cold.

Salmon and Asparagus Salad. Arrange cold boiled asparagus that is tender on a large platter or flat dish, with the tips outward if possible. Season with a French dressing or sprinkle with oil, vinegar, salt and pepper if more convenient. Pile the flaked salmon in the centre of the platter or dish sprinkling with a little lemon juice if the fish is too dry. Put in an ice chest until perfectly cold and, just before serving, pour mayonnaise dressing over the fish.

Salmon and Green Pea Salad is made the same as asparagus salad using green peas with the salmon.

Russian Salmon Salad. What is called salmon salad *a la Russe* is made by decorating a mound with tails of crayfish, hard boiled eggs, truffles, oysters, etc., as well as cold boiled vegetables cut into fancy shapes, dipped into strong aspic jelly to hold them in place and then filling the mound with cold boiled salmon and a clear, highly flavored aspic jelly, cucumber jelly being the favorite. When hard and cold, turn out of the mound and serve in a platter with mayonnaise dressing poured around it.

French Fish Salad. A favorite way with our Gallic friends is to cut nice slices from cold boiled fish, three or four inches long and place them on plates of lettuce: over that is poured a heaping tablespoonful of mayonnaise dressing in which sardines ground and mashed have been stirred, or a sardine boned and freed from skin is laid on the slice of fish before the dressing is put on. Minced parsley, chervil, basil, fennel or any salad herb preferred can be sprinkled over the top. The sardine flavor is an addition when the fish is flat or weak in flavor but with salmon, horse mackerel or any rich, highly flavored fish had better be omitted.

Spanish Fish Salad. Arrange on individual plates, or in a salad dish, boiled fish on lettuce, then a layer of sweet pepper shredded as fine as possible, hard boiled eggs and olives sliced. Serve with French dressing made with onion juice, or if made in a salad bowl, the bowl can be rubbed with garlic.

Anchovy Salad. The bottled anchovies are the best to use if they are obtainable. If salted anchovies are to be used soak them in cold water for about two hours or until they are well freshened, they drain and dry them and remove the skin, bones etc., dividing the meat into small pieces and squeezing the juice of a lemon over it. Mix with lettuce or celery cut into rather small pieces. Hard boiled eggs should be cut up and mixed with lettuce and fish, nearly as much egg as fish. Cold boiled potatoes, string beans, sliced raw onions and other vegetables are often added. Serve with French dressing made with onion juice or tartare sauce. Six to eight salt anchovies are enough for an ordinary salad but if small or bottled ones are used more are required.

Sardine Salad. Sardine, salad can be made with either lettuce or celery with a sprinkling of any other fine herb that will be relished for flavoring. To one small box of sardines, two good stalks of celery or an equal quantity of lettuce is about the right proportion. If the oil in which the sardines is packed is poor, drain it carefully off and

scrape away with the skin and bones of the fish, but if
the oil is of good quality most people like a little of it
mixed with the salad. Use mayonnaise or French dressing.
If mayonnaise is used the salad looks well served in a flat
glass dish or platter. Like all fish salads it harmonizes well
with hard boiled eggs but all fish salads should not be gar
nished alike.

Salt Codfish Salad. Take about half of an ordinary
sized salt codfish and soak over night in plenty of water.
Dry and cut away the fins etc., rub with butter and broil.
When cold pick out the meat and divide into quarter inch
pieces. Put in a bowl and cover with French dressing letting
it stand an hour. Mix with crisp lettuce and serve with
mayonnaise or French dressing. Salt salmon may be used
in the same way. Another method of preparing is to
broil the fish as directed and put in a bowl finely divided
with a little more than the same quantity of hot potatoes
sliced: pour over it a claret glass of Rhine wine, cover and
allow it to cool. When ready to serve add a few endive
leaves. Dress with a French dressing and serve. Boiled
codfish may be used in the same way but is not so good.
Still another way is to soak the fish to remove the salt and
then, for a family salad, pick about a cupful into fine
shreds. Cut an onion into a pan with a tablespoonful of
butter and cook until browned.: then add the fish and
cook very slowly for a few minutes. If too dry add enough
water to keep it quite moist. Shredded green pepper can
be added to the onion if liked. When cold arrange in a
salad bowl with tomatoes, peeled and sliced, or lettuce, and
dress with French dressing.

Eel Salad is best made with endive. Pick the meat from
cooked or potted eels and add to it an equal quantity of
bleached endive, Serve with remoulade dressing. Garnish
with lemon, pickled oysters, crabs, shrimp, etc.

Whitebait Salad. The little fish that are sold as white.

bait are the fry of nearly all large fish according to the locality in which they are caught. Mackerel, shad, herring, smelt, black-fish, weak-fish are the most common. When wanted for salad, after being well washed and wiped, dredge them with flour and fry in a kettle of hot boiling fat. Drain, cool and serve with lettuce and mayonnaise dressing or tartare sauce.

Sheepshead or " Scup " Salad. Either of these fish or those of similar character make good salads boiled with flavoring herbs or vinegar. When cold, remove the white meat, divide into flakes and mix with crisp lettuce and mayonnaise dressing. If preferred the meat may be given a marinade of Worcestershire sauce diluted with vinegar and then mixed with lettuce and remoulade dressing. Crab or lobster meat, shrimp, etc., are good for garnishing.

Fisherman's Salad. This is often acceptable on the water or in camp. Take the proportions of two pounds of cooked fish in clean meat, one of cold boiled potatoes and half a head of cold cabbage using, if possible, both the red and white cabbage. Finely chopped pickles or cucumbers added are good. Serve with any good dressing available. A liberal supply of pepper is usually relished when this salad is eaten in the open air.

Halibut Salad, is one of the best of fish salads. Have boiled halibut and add one half its bulk of lettuce or celery, or, to one quarter the quantity of halibut add one quarter boiled cauliflower or potatoes. Viniagrette Sauce, Sardine dressing, Hollandaise sauce, Anchovy dressing or plain French dressing with or without onions are all good for use with this salad.

Lake Trout Salad. The larger salmon or lake trout can be served in salads like salmon, or they can be boiled in water slightly salted to which a little vinegar or half the quantity of acid wine has been added. Herbs, sliced onions etc., can be added to the water but avoid destroying the flavor of the fish by over seasoning. Let the fish drain and cool, then pick the meat out carefully and mix with good lettuce, French or mayonnaise dressing.

Brook Trout Salad. When this delightful fish is available for salad it is most excellent prepared in the following manner. Boil the fish in salted water to which a little vinegar or acid wine has been added and any flavoring herb desired, cool and drain: then split each fish down the back, being careful not to break the fish, remove all bones, but not the head, keeping the natural shape of the fish. When ready to serve, have, on separate plates, nicely arranged, lettuce carefully dressed with French dressing.

Turbot Salad can be made the same as sole or flounder salad and is, perhaps, better than either. Any of the directions for boiled fish salads can be carried out with turbot.

Smelt Salad. The peculiar taste that smelt have at times is relished by some and disliked by others but nearly every one likes the fish when made into salad. There are more elaborate salads in use than those here given but they are not adapted to American use. Boil a dozen smelt fifteen minutes, drain and cool, then remove the meat from all the bones and cut in half inch pieces. Arrange in a salad bowl with two crisp heads of lettuce and sprinkle with two salted anchovies, minced fine. Serve with mild mayonnaise or remoulade sauce.

Salad of Smelts. An old English Recipe. Take fifty smelt of large size that have been cleaned, drawn and heads cut off and put them to soak in a pint of white wine vinegar, or sufficient to cover them when packed close. Put among them one onion and two sliced lemons, a race of ginger, three or four blades of mace, a nutmeg sliced or crushed, a dozen whole black peppers and a spoonful of salt. Let them stand covered at least twenty-four hours:

if desired to keep them for some days see that the vinegar is not too strong for the taste, diluting, if necessary. When wanted for use remove from the pickle, scrape, split open and cut out all the bones. Arrange on a dish with open sides up and sprinkle with the grated yellow rind of orange or lemon and chopped parsley, fine pepper and lemon juice. Pour on a good quantity of salad oil and let them stand for some time to absorb all the oil they will.

Sole or Flounder Salad. Boil four or five pounds of the fish, a single large fish is best, and let it get quite cold then remove the white meat carefully from the skin and bones, divide it into flakes and cover with a marinade of French dressing, let it remain half an hour and then drain. When ready to serve mix with lettuce and remoulade sauce or put the fish on leaves of lettuce and pour a spoonful of dressing over it. Very small little neck clams, oyster crabs or shrimp are good for garnishing.

Bloater Salad. Remove the skin and bones from two Yarmouth bloaters that have been boiled or broiled, and cut the meat into shreds. Mix in a salad bowl with two good sized boiled potatoes, sliced small, a head of bleached endive, minced capers and a few minced fresh herbs if they can be had. Chopped anchovies are sometimes added. French dressing is used with this salad.

Tropical Fish Salad. Fish salad is made in South America and other warm climates by cleaning the fish, splitting it and then covering it with lemon or lime juice and letting it remain for twelve hours. The fish is cooked by the action of the acid, the bones and skin carefully taken out and the fish served with lettuce or shredded cabbage palm and a French or remoulade dressing.

Shell Fish Salads.

THE various shell fish obtainable in almost all parts of this country, provide us with material for salad making which, to say the least, adds variety to the list of favorite salads. Shell fish salads are especially desirable in hot weather and they always acquire an additional flavor when the fish are caught by one's self. Along the sea shore, in the various rivers running into the ocean, "crabbing" is one of the delightful occupations of summer visitors, which reaches its most complete enjoyment when the day's catch is served in one of the several delicious ways.

LOBSTER SALADS.

Salads made with lobsters are the most generally approved of all fish salads. They are among the easiest to make but alas! one of the most rare to find good, either on public or private tables. Too great elaboration and the use of too high seasoning are the common faults. Nothing can be finer than the natural relish and delicate flavoring of fresh lobster, and all our efforts should tend to preserve and accentuate instead of diminishing or obscuring its delicacy.

Medium sized lobsters are to be preferred, for large ones are often tough while small ones have little meat and are generally soft and tasteless from too long boiling. Lobsters can always be bought fresh and well boiled at the fish markets and are usually better by being boiled in large numbers. If the lobsters are uncooked, boil from thirty to forty-five minutes as they are large or small, and when cold pick out the meat carefully from the shells rejecting the stomach and sand pouch as well as the intestines that run through the tail.

If one is not familiar with the formation of the lobster it is best to get instruction from some experienced person in breaking the shell and extracting the meat. Take time in doing this work and be careful to save all the green fat, and scrape off that which adhers to the inside of the shells. The more delicate and highly flavored parts are usually thrown away in hotels and restaurants because it saves the servants time and avoids trouble: the consequent result is the abomination usually served as lobster salad. It is said that *chefs* are scarce who do not claim that they can make a better salad than any one else but he who can make a better one than number one here given is a genius.

Lobster Salad No. 1. Pick the meat carefully from the shells being careful that no small pieces of shell gets among it. Cut the large pieces up into half inch bits, but not smaller or the dish will have a heavy sodden look. Sprinkle lightly with fine salt and when ready to serve mix with a little more than its own bulk of crisp lettuce torn into convenient sized pieces. Pour over the whole a mayonnaise dressing made with mustard and into which the fat of the lobster has been beaten. Mix lightly just before serving so that each guest will get the proper proportion of both salad and dressing.

Avoid elaborate garnishes. Put a few well-formed leaves of lettuce around the edges of the plates and sprinkle the coral or eggs of the lobster, broken into fine bits, over the top. Nothing can be more attractive than the scarlet and white of the fish with the green and cream of the lettuce. Let no one persuade you to put vinegar or anything but a little salt on the lobster meat. If more acid is wanted sprinkle a little lemon juice or vinegar over the lettuce.

The claws and parts of the shell are often used as an attractive garnish but they make it awkward in helping and mixing and are untidy on the table. Stoned olives, sliced beets, capers etc., are commonly added but should not be

mixed with the salad. Let them be served on a separate
dish if wanted, each guest helping himself. Hard boiled
eggs harmonize in taste and can be used to increase the
quantity of salad if necessary. Serve good bread and butter with this salad, and on no account let the salad stand
long after the dressing is mixed with it.

Lobster Salad No. 2. (*a 'L' Allemand.*) Pick out the meat
of the lobster and arrange on a bed of lettuce or on individual plates. Sprinkle plentifully with finely minced parsley and the yolks of hard boiled eggs pressed through a
sieve. When ready to serve cover with French dressing.

Lobster Salad No. 3. (*a la Boardman.*) Pick the meat
from two medium sized lobsters, cut into pieces and put in
a salad bowl with three hard boiled eggs chopped fine.
Peel and chop very fine two small sound shallots (or onions)
add one and one half teaspoonfuls parsley, one small head
of sound celery. Put all these finely chopped herbs in a
bowl with the lobster meat and season with a tablespoonful
of salt, one and a half of oil, two of vinegar, and half teaspoonful white or black pepper, same of Worcestershire
sauce. Add three tablespoonfuls mayonnaise sauce and
thoroughly and gently mix the whole.

Lobster Salad No. 4. (*a la Mexicano.*) This is the best
salad when canned lobster must be used. Shrimp and other
shell fish can be dressed in the same way. Cut up one
pound of lobster meat coarsely and sprinkle with fine salt.
Put in a salad bowl with one tart apple sliced, one minced
Spanish pepper and lettuce or celery as wished. Pour over
it a French dressing.

Lobster Salad No. 5. (*a la Russe.*) Line a salad bowl
with lettuce and heap upon it lobster meat and about the
same quantity each of young boiled carrots and beets cut
into small cubes, and mixed with mayonnaise dressing. Put
more mayonnaise on, coloring it if wished and mix with a
little Russian Cavaire,

Lobster Salad No. 6. (Broiled.) Split and broil live lobsters, pick the meat out and cut into half inch pieces. When still warm dip into melted butter and a little vinegar and then into Chili sauce. When cold and ready to serve mix with lettuce and dress with remoulade sauce or with Chili sauce alone

Crab Salad—Hard Shell. Boil the crabs by plunging in hot salted water to remain for twenty or twenty-five min· utes. When cold pick out the meat and treat as for lobster salad. It is usually preferred treated as with lobster salad number one. Do not obscure the delicacy of the crabs by strong seasoning. Remoulade sauce is the approved form of mayonnaise to use with this salad.

Crab Salad—Soft Shell. Fry as usual, or better still broil the crabs after putting a little oil on them. Cool and cut into pieces of convenient size removing any hard or defective parts. Mix with lettuce and serve with mayonnaise, remoulade or tartare sauce. A few pickled mussels or oysters make a good garnish.

Shrimp or Prawn Salad. This is made the same as any of the lobster or crab salads, that with lettuce and mayonnaise being the best. If the shrimp are dry or salted soak in clear water until soft and fresh. Fresh shrimp require considerable salt. Examine carefully and see that no pieces of the thin shell remain in the mixture. Always have the salad as cold as possible.

Shrimp Salad with Tomatoes. One can or one quart of fresh shrimp is required. Boil fresh shrimp fifteen minutes in salted water. Throw canned shrimp in cold water to soften for a few minutes. Pick out all pieces of shell carefully, drain and put in a cold place. Peel four to six smooth sound ripe tomatoes. Place all in a cool place. When ready to serve, slice the tomatoes and arrange prettily with the shrimp and pour over a mayonnaise dressing.

Salad a Croquet. Shrimp salad made with water cresses is a croquet. Pick over carefully a good handful of the cress adding the leaves to the salad with any mild dressing liked.

Cray Fish Salad. Cray-fish are excellent for salad and like shrimp are much appreciated if they can be had where lobsters, crabs and other salt water crustaceans do not abound. Wash and boil in salted water for fifteen or twenty minutes. When cold remove the meat from the shells dividing that from the tails and removing the intestines. Place in a salad bowl with an equal quantity of lettuce and dress with mayonnaise. Hard boiled eggs or any garnish may be used with them. These directions are equally serviceable for the salt water cray-fish or the small ones found in fresh water.

Mussel Salad. Wash and boil in the shells for five minutes, remove from the shells and dip in hot melted butter seasoned with salt, pepper and lemon juice. Cool and when ready to serve mix with lettuce and a French dressing. Thin buttered slices of Boston brown bread are good with this salad and any other made of shell fish.

The most attractive way to serve a salad of oysters, clams, scallops etc., is in a bowl made of ice with the centre melted out with a hot iron. Stand in a large platter to catch the drip from the ice. Decorate with any pretty green. Serve the oysters with a little ladle on plates of shredded cabbage, celery, lettuce etc. Have the fish cold when put in the ice.

Oyster Salad No. 1. Scald the oysters lightly in their own liquor only long enough to make them plump and frilled. Let them drain and get very cold. When ready to serve mix with mayonnaise, French dressing or tartare sauce and lay each portion on plates of lettuce or mix the oysters with lettuce or celery cut rather fine using a salad.

bowl to mix in. For salads the small oysters are always preferred the large ones requiring to be cut which detracts from their appearance.

Oyster Salad No. 2. Boil for five minutes two or three dozen small oysters with sufficient of their liquor or water to cover them: add a tablespoonful of vinegar and a little salt if the oysters are fresh. Drain and cool. Put in a salad bowl with one large or two small heads of lettuce torn to pieces, pour over all a mayonnaise and garnish with oyster crabs, stuffed olives or capers.

Oyster Salad No. 3. Mix in a salad bowl one quart of cold raw oysters with two large heads of celery cut into quarter inch pieces. Pour over these, and just before helping mix all together, the following dressing. The yolks of three raw eggs and two yolks of hard boiled, with two or three tablespoonfuls of sweet oil, one small teaspoonful of salt, half a teaspoonful of black pepper and made English mustard. Stir until smooth and even and then thin by dropping in, while stirring hard, about four tablespoonfuls of good vinegar or lemon juice.

Oyster Salad No. 4. For a small salad take two or three dozen cold raw oysters well drained, and an equal bulk of sweet raw cabbage cut into shreds: if preferred celery may be used but cabbage is generally liked best. Dust salt over the cabbage and add just enough sweet oil to coat it when well mixed. Mix with the juice of one lemon a teaspoonful of grated horseradish, five drops of tobasco sauce and pour over the oysters. Just before serving, the oysters and cabbage can be mixed but a better way is to have two bowls one holding the oysters, the other the cabbage and when serving place a portion of cabbage at each place and then with a small ladle put a few oysters over the cabbage or at the side of it.

Clams or Oysters with Fish Salad. Take equal parts

of cold boiled fish and oysters, soft or hard shell clams raw
or slightly cooked removing the black heads. Cold clams
from a Rhode Island clam bake are good to use in this way
but the hard shell or little neck clams are best uncooked.
Mix with crisp lettuce in a salad bowl and serve with
French dressing.

Salad of Little Neck Clams. A most refreshing salad
can be made with the hard shell clams or quahaugs called
in the market little neck clams. Small ones look best but
the large ones taste quite as well. Cut into small pieces
and mix with twice the bulk of good lettuce using a French
dressing with a few drops of onion juice or, if preferred,
the dressing described for oyster salad number four. A
little chopped fresh sweet basil harmonizes delightfully with
the flavor of clams.

Salad of Bong or Soft Shell Clams. Boil or roast the
clams just long enough to make them firm and come out of
their shell easily, or take cold clams from a Rhode Island
clam bake cut off the black heads and remove all skin.
Serve with lettuce and mayonnaise, plain dressing or any of
those given for oyster salads.

Scallop Salad—Cooked. Soak the scallops in cold salted
water for an hour or and then cook in boiling salted water
for five minutes: drain and cool. When cold slice them if
preferred and sprinkle with good white vinegar. When
ready to serve drain off the vinegar and arrange the scallops in a nest of lettuce leaves, shredded cabbage or celery
and cover them with mayonnaise dressing. Capers or thin
slices of pickled peppers or gherhins are nice to serve with
them.

Scallop Salad—Raw. Serve cold as possible with an
equal quantity of lettuce or shredded cabbage and a French
dressing. If preferred use the dressing recommended in
oyster salad number four. If the scallops seem too fresh
salt them slightly.

Scallop Salad—Fried. Fry as usual and if large cut in halves. Mix with two-thirds their bulk of cut celery and mayonnaise dressing.

Luncheon Salad of Conchs. About three pounds of conchs, alive, are put into boiling water for about five minutes or just long enough to loosen them from their shells: long boiling makes them tough. Cut into medium sized pieces and when cold serve in a salad bowl with lettuce and a mayonnaise dressing. Capers and olives cut up and mixed with it is an improvement. Garnish with lettuce and cucumbers. Conchs are found on many parts of our coast and are offered in season in the large city fish markets.

Tame and Wild Fowl Salads.

SALADS made from the flesh of either tame or wild fowls are especially favored by Americans and with reason. The American housekeeper assuredly possesses the knack of cooking fowl in a manner which renders it especially appetizing, yet retaining all the delicacy of flavor.

Chicken Salad. This is justly regarded as an American dainty, for owing to some reason which cannot be explained, it is never found in perfection anywhere else and often times even in this country is not what it should be. Over-elaboration is the usual fault in preparation and too much acid in the dressing which destroys the delicacy of the flavor and, in public places, gives rise to the suspicion that it is used to disguise a disagreeable taste. Much nonsense has been written about chicken salad and many recipes, especially foreign ones, are misleading. Chicken salad is in perfection during the fall and winter because chicken and celery are at their best then. When celery is not to be had lettuce may be substituted but is never as good. Crisp cabbage may also be used. Boiled chicken is always best for salad making but the remains of almost any roast fowl are acceptable dressed in this way.

The best chicken salad is made by boiling the fowls until tender and then letting them remain in the water until nearly or quite cold, which will prevent the meat from being too dry. This can be done the day before the birds are wanted for use. When cold and well drained, pick the white meat from the bones, carefully rejecting all pieces of skin, dark meat and bones, and cut into pieces about half an inch square. Sprinkle with fine salt and put on ice. Cut only the white and tender parts of celery into pieces

about a quarter of an inch thick, rejecting any that is dark
and tough. Have one-third chicken meat and two-thirds celery, as a rule, though more chicken is often allowed. When
ready to serve mix with a liberal allowance of mild mayonnaise and serve as soon as possible thereafter. The cold-
er it is, short of being frozen, the better it will be. It is
customary to decorate chicken salads with hard boiled eggs,
slices of pickled beets and stoned olives, but as the taste of
some of these garnishings may be disagreeable to some of
the guests, it is best not to mix them in the salad but to
serve the sliced beets, olives and capers, if used, separately.
The dark meat of the chicken is quite as good as the white
meat but had better be made in a separate salad in the
same way as the white meat, and used if more is wanted.

Italian Chicken Salad. Take the white meat of two
chickens and divide into long flakes : pile in the centre of a
flat dish and arrange a border of lettuce around it. Arrange the whites of three hard boiled eggs cut into rings in
a chain-like pattern, on the lettuce. Make a dressing with
the yolks of the eggs, a mustardspoonful of made mustard,
about as much paprika or a little Cayenne, a small teaspoonful of fine sugar, four tablespoonfuls of oil and one of
vinegar. Cook in a bowl on top of a kettle or use a double
boiler, but do not allow it to boil. When cold pour over
the chicken or serve in a separate dish.

Swiss Chicken Salad. To the meat of one cooked chicken
take one cucumber chopped, one teacup English walnuts
chopped, one can French peas and two heads of celery cut
small. Mayonnaise dressing.

Aspic with Chicken and Walnuts To every three cupfuls of clear, strong chicken *consomme* (which can be made
from the water chickens are boiled in for salad) add a box
of sparkling gelatine that has been soaked in a cupful of
water, salt to taste and add a little Cayenne. Have celery
cut rather fine, and one-quarter the quantity of celery in the

meat of English walnuts blanched, cut into pieces the same size of the celery and dressed with three tablespoonfuls of the jelly, two of oil, one teaspoonful of salt, two of vinegar and a little pepper. Have a double mould and when the jelly is hard fill the centre with the celery mixture leaving space enough for more liquid jelly so as to completely cover the celery. Place on ice, turn out and serve when very cold. Arrange with lettuce or white celery tops. Cold turkey with oysters and pieces of acid orange can be used for filling. Boiled chestnuts and pieces of boiled chicken liver can also be introduced if desired.

Turkey Salad. Cold turkey makes an excellent salad, made in exactly the same way as chicken salad. In boiling use as little water as possible. The water from clams or oysters is excellent to boil a turkey in if diluted somewhat. Stewed or boiled chestnuts are good to mix with the salad. If cold roast turkey is to be used the meat is often too dry and should be moistened with oil and vinegar, three spoonfuls of oil and one of vinegar, and allowed to stand a little before mixing.

Turkey Salad with Chestnuts and Apples. Take the dark meat from the side bones and second joints of a fair sized turkey, cut into half inch pieces and sprinkle lightly with salt. Have the meat from two dozen large or twice as many small American chestnuts, that have been boiled twenty minutes and then shelled, put in cold water to remove the inner brown skin. Cut into halves or quarters and salt lightly. Peel and slice four good sized crisp acid apples, when ready for the salad and mix with the chestnuts and turkey meat. Dress with French dressing or mayonnaise, the French being preferred. Lettuce makes a good garnish and some people like the addition of minced pickles.

Goose Salad. A rich salad can be made from the remains of a roast goose in winter, or a young green goose in summer. Cut the meat into long thin strips, carefully remove all skin and fat. In winter mix with an equal quantity of shredded celery and crisp acid apples and dress with mayonnaise. A sprinkle of sage is a desirable addition to the taste, or sage sandwiches can be served with the salad. The boiled liver can be salted and use for garnishing. Salt the meat if too fresh.

Partridge Salad—American. Salads of game are not so popular in America as in foreign countries for we usually prefer our game broiled or roasted, and served with some simple and appropriately seasoned salad, instead of being made into an elaborate compound to astonish the palate. Yet when game is plenty new ways to serve it are desired and the remains of a game supper can often be utilized in a palatable yet economical manner.

Cut the meat from a cold roasted partridge into cubes about one-half inch in diameter leaving out all bones and skin. Add a minced cucumber pickle, one teaspoonful of chopped parsley, pour over it a French dressing and let it stand an hour: then add the torn leaves of a head of lettuce or three heads of celery. cut up, and serve. Mayonnaise dressing can be added if wanted.

Partridge Salad—English. Cut a roasted partridge into eight or ten pieces and arrange in the centre of a platter on a bed of lettuce, celery, cress or any green that is in season. Make a thin flat border of butter about an inch from the edge of the platter. Have eight cold hard boiled eggs cut into pieces and arrange together the white and yellow pieces alternating. Prepare a dressing as follows. Beat together a tablespoonful of finely chopped shallots, onions or chives, one of fine sugar, one teaspoonful of chopped parsley, tarragon or chervil, the raw yolk of one egg, quarter of an ounce of salt, and a little Cayenne pepper. Mix in, by degrees, four tablespoonfuls of oil and two of vinegar, or pepper sauce if preferred. Put on ice and when ready to serve whip with a gill of rich cream, pour over the partridge and serve.

Grouse Salad—English. Roast the grouse and prepare a salmi sauce with the trimmings. Reduce it stiffly and mix in about one-third of aspic jelly. Cut the birds into convenient pieces to serve and dip each into the sauce giving each a thick coating. Put on ice to harden. Put a a thick bed of shredded lettuce in a dish and upon it pile the pieces of jellied grouse. Garnish with quarters of hard boiled eggs and celery tops. Pour white mayonnaise over the pieces of bird.

Grouse Salad a la Soyer is prepared like American Partridge salad using grouse instead of partridge.

Pigeon Salad. Both the wild and domestic birds can be made into good salads. Roast the pigeons and when cold pick the meat from the bones and cut into convenient pieces. Sprinkle a little salt over it and if dry let it soak in a marinade made in the proportions of one spoonful of vinegar to three of oil. When the salad is wanted, mix with lettuce or celery and serve with a mayonnaise dressing. A French dressing in which a few crushed leaves of summer savory, marjoram, thyme or other sweet herbs have been soaking will be preferred by many.

Quail Salad is made the same as pigeon salad, with lettuce. Let the meat which is usually dry stand in a marinade of French dressing before mixing.

Pea-Fowl Salad. In the warmer portions of our country where pea fowl are often plentiful the meat of a cold bird can be most acceptably served as a salad. The meat is usually dry and if a roasted fowl is used it should be put in a marinade which may be spiced and flavored with herbs if desired although too high seasoning disguises the peculiar flavor of the meat. Mix with lettuce or shredded celery to which is often added boiled chestnuts cut into small pieces, and raisins stoned and chopped. Dress with mayonnaise dressing, without mustard, garnish with small moulds or pieces of acid lemon, currant or cranberry jelly serving a piece to each guest. If the dish containing the salad is placed on another flat one in which are arranged some of the gay feathers of the bird, it can be made quite a feature in any entertainment.

Guinea-Fowl Salad. Cut the meat of cold roasted birds into one-half inch pieces and mix with a little more than the same quantity of lettuce or celery and serve with mayonnaise dressing. Acid jellies, sections of sour oranges, capers etc., are excellent to serve with it.

A Polish Salad. One quart cold game or poultry meat cut fine, moistened with French dressing and allowed to stand in a cool place for several hours. When wanted shred a large head of lettuce into long narrow strips, place on a dish and pile the meat in the centre. Chop four hard boiled eggs fine and sprinkle over the whole. If too dry, more dressing may be added.

Supreme Salad. This salad is also attributed to Poland, and is made by cutting cold roast game, roast goose or any other domestic fowl into small dice and mixing with an equal quantity of cold boiled potatoes cut up in the same way. These are arranged in layers, sprinkled with pepper, salt and finely minced chives and over all is poured a dressing made of equal parts of oil and vinegar with mustard to suit the taste. The salad is allowed to stand and absorb the dressing before being served.

Various Egg Salads.

S OME people have an uncontrollable fondness for accompanying all kinds of salads with hard boiled eggs. This is a mistake as it gives sameness where variety is desirable. Eggs harmonize in taste with all salads made of fowls or fish, but seem out of place with meats, excepting when forming a part of the dressing. When eggs are abundant and fresh a good salad may be made with almost any kind of salad herb and eggs. Duck's eggs and those of geese and any wild fowl are also good for salads. Those of sea fowl will require pungent seasonings. The use of the eggs of game birds is to be discouraged.

Plain Egg Salad. Boil the eggs fifteen or twenty minutes and let them get perfectly cold before cutting. Slice them over crisp lettuce, sprinkle lightly with salt and serve with French dressing. Celery can be used instead of lettuce. Chopped cresses are a good addition and cottage or cream cheese a good accompaniment.

Egg Salad with Cabbage. Boil six eggs hard. When cold cut in two evenly and take out the yolks. Mix these in a soup plate with a tablespoonful of melted butter, salt, a sprinkle of Cayenne pepper and half a teaspoonful of made mustard: form into little balls and fill the space in the whites from which the yolks were taken. Shred up as much white cabbage as is wanted and season with vinegar, pepper and salt. Place in the bottom of a dish and arrange the parts of egg on it. Sprinkle with chopped parsley or cress and serve with boiled dressing or mayonnaise.

Floral Egg Salad. Arrange a bed of lettuce leaves on a flat round dish, the stems toward the centre: cover the middle with mayonnaise dressing and place on this hard boiled eggs cut in quarters and arranged with their sides to each other like the petals of a sunflower, leaving space in the centre for a bunch of nasturtium flowers, white endive, cowslips etc. Serve a little more mayonnaise if the dish does not hold a sufficient quantity to go round.

Egg and Sardine Salad. Cut into a salad bowl, in narrow strips, two good sized heads of celery, shredding the whites of three hard boiled eggs with them. Mash the yolks with the meat of four sardines, a little salt and pepper. Stir in cream enough to make a thick paste and thin with a little vinegar. Sprinkle salt over the celery and white of egg, with pepper if liked, toss about and pour the dressing over it.

Egg and Sweet Herb Salad. Cut hard boiled eggs in halves, lengthwise. Sprinkle with salt, a little Cayenne pepper and add a few drops of oil and vinegar to each piece of yolk. Arrange on lettuce or cress and scatter chopped chives, chervil and tarragon over the whole.

" Columbus " Salad. Have as many hard boiled eggs as are needed, cut them in halves, neatly remove the yolk and keep the whites in form so that they may be fitted together again. Mix the yolks with mayonnaise dressing, finely chopped boiled tongue, chicken or ham, adding a little lemon juice, butter, salt and pepper. Or, mix with minced anchovies or sardines seasoning with oil, vinegar, salt and pepper, onion or minced chives. Fill the hollows in the centre of the whites of the eggs with one of the mixtures, re-unite the halves making them look like whole eggs. Cut a little piece from one end of each egg so that it will stand on end, a la Columbus, and arrange them on endive or lettuce serving with any dressing liked. Any of the yolk mixture remaining may be made into small sandwiches to serve with the salad. If preferred, each white of egg may be filled with a round ball like the original yolk and arranged without uniting the halves.

Egg and Potato Salad. Take hard boiled eggs and cold boiled potatoes, about one third potato, salt and mix with chopped capers and parsley or any herb that is liked and serve with mayonnaise dressing.

Water Lily Salad. Cut hard boiled egg into pieces lengthwise and trim a little to resemble the petals of a pond lily. Large and small eggs can be used for the inner and outer rows. Arrange to resemble the flower, on a round leaf of lettuce, with the centre of the flower formed of the broken yolks of eggs. Place on a flat glass dish to simulate water, and trim lettuce into the shape of leaves forming the stems with the stalks of the coarser leaves trimmed close. Before cutting some of the eggs they can be colored a delicate pink by standing, while hot, in warm beet juice and water. Serve separately any kind of dressing.

Egg Salad with Cream Cheese. (*Salade au Nid.*) Take the yolks of hard boiled eggs and rub to a paste with an equal quantity of Neufchatel cream cheese. Season with salt, paprika or Cayenne pepper and make into egg shape balls. Arrange lettuce upon a dish and shred the whites of the eggs as fine as possible, make a nest of them upon the lettuce and place the cheese balls in it. About ten minutes before helping pour over it a white mayonnaise dressing.

Egg and Celery Salad. Arrange hard boiled eggs and cut celery into any pretty way fancied and dress with mayonnaise.

Egg and Parsley Salad. Wash thoroughly and chop fine a sufficient quantity of young, tender and fresh parsley: spread on a platter and on this place hard boiled eggs cut in slices, salt and eat with French dressing.

Meat Salads.

PROBABLY more scraps of meat are wasted in the average household than is generally realized: not, of course, deliberately wasted, but because so little of some particular kind is left over from a meal it seems impossible to utilize it to advantage. Then too, there is the desire for a change from the inevitable roasted or boiled meats. There are numerous ways in which delicious salads may be made of several kinds of meat and give us at once a change and a delicious meal.

Lamb Salad. Take cold roast lamb cut in small slices or half inch cubes, one pound of meat to two large heads of lettuce. Sprinkle with a dozen chopped capers. French or remoulade dressing. A little chopped mint may be added if the taste is relished.

Lamb's Tongue Salad. Allow one large cold boiled potato to three cooked and pickled lamb's tongues. Add lettuce and endive if desired. Sprinkle with chopped parsley on the sliced potato and tongue and serve with French dressing.

Beef Salads. There are various excellent ways in which to serve cold beef for a quick lunch that will extend a small quantity of good meat much farther than if served by itself. Number one is very popular as a "business lunch" in New York.

Number 1. Cut cold roast beef into small even slices but not so thin they will lose their shape, and serve with plain potato salad made with French dressing and onions.

Number 2. Cut the well done portions of cold roast beef,

65

without the fat, into small pieces and marinade with enough plain dressing to flavor it: let it stand and when wanted mix with an equal quantity of endivé or lettuce any mixed herbs wanted and more French dressing. Boiled vegetables, beets, potatoes or cauliflower may be used instead of lettuce.

Number 3. Shred a sweet Spanish pepper fine and mix with one large head of lettuce torn up and half a pound of cold beef cut into small pieces. French or mayonnaise dressing.

Number 4. Take boiled beef, cut into half inch cubes and marinade, using French dressing made with onion juice. Mix with an equal quantity of cold boiled potatoes cut the same way, more French dressing or mayonnaise and chopped parsley.

Number 5. (*Solpicon de Carne.*) Take cold boiled beef cut into half inch cubes, boil and chop an onion and add it to the meat, or slice the onion raw, soak it in vinegar and then add to the meat with chopped olives, fresh marjoram and parsley. French dressing.

Number 6. For a salad of ordinary size press the vinegar from four tablespoonfuls of prepared horseradish, add a little salt and a few drops of onion juice and mix with six tablespoonfuls of thick cream whipped to a froth. Arrange the beef on lettuce leaves, pour over the dressing and serve at once. If the cream is not at hand mix a little water with the vinegar and scatter over the beef, letting it stand until absorbed and then serve with mayonnaise dressing.

Beef to eat with Salad. Take a round of fresh beef weighing ten or twelve pounds, lard it with strips of salt pork rolled in pepper and a very little ground clove, then place in a large frying pan and fry in lard on all sides and the ends. This prevents the juice from escaping. Cover the bottom of a large porcelain-lined pot with the coarse green leaves of celery that can be used for no other purpose. Put in the beef and stuff celery tops and leaves all around the sides and on top until the pot is full. Throw in a large spoonful of salt, fill with cold water and boil slowly until perfectly tender, then take out and press. To be eaten cold with salad. The boiling will take from three to five hours according to the tenderness of the beef: as no rule can be given the meat should be tried frequently with a fork: it should be perfectly tender but not so that it will fall apart. The beef can be cut into slices and mixed with the salad, but the more elegant way is to have it handsomely garnished with celery leaves on a platter, cut into slices and put on plates with the salad as it is served.

Tripe Salad. Those who like tripe will enjoy it made in one of the following excellent forms. Cut into half inch pieces boiled or pickled tripe: if boiled squeeze over it the juice of a lemon. Sprinkle with chopped olives and parsley and dress with French dressing made with onion juice and a few leaves of sweet marjoram crushed and allowed to remain in the oil some time before mixing.

Another way is to take equal quantities of tripe, boiled potatoes and endive cut up into half inch pieces seasoning with French dressing and capers. Or, take one-third tripe with two-thirds sliced celery and mayonnaise dressing.

Veal Salad. Veal is a favorite meat with many people. When used as a salad it is usually substituted for or mixed with chicken in chicken salad. Be careful to have the veal well and thoroughly done and carefully reject all pieces of gristle as well as brown or hard portions. One half each of cold veal and fine chopped white cabbage with mayonnaise or horseradish dressing is a favorite salad. Cut well done cold veal into half inch pieces and marinade or soak in oil and vinegar for two hours. then dress with three tablespoonfuls of oil, one of vinegar, one teaspoonful of

French mustard, two of pounded anchovies or anchovy
sauce. If not salt enough sprinkle fine salt over the veal
and add chopped pickles and capers. Mustard leaves, par
sley etc., can be added if wanted.

Calf's Head Salad No. 1. Take the tongue and one side
of a cold boiled calf's head, cut into pieces about three-
eights of an inch across and marinade in a French dressing
to which horseradish can be added. See that all tough or
unpleasant looking pieces are removed. Cut into small cubes
two medium size cold boiled potatoes and about an equal
quantity of cold boiled beets and carrots. If not salt enough
sprinkle lightly with fine salt. Arrange on a dish with the
meat in the centre, the vegetables forming a border. Sprink-
a cupful of crisp water cress leaves over it. A little chick-
ory, endive or Romaine lettuce will be a welcome addition.
When ready mix all together with mayonnaise dressing.

Calf's Head Salad No. 2. This salad is thought by many
to be superior to all other salads. Use cold boiled calf's
head cut into half inch pieces using the tongue and a portion of the outside part, carefully rejecting all but the se-
lected portions. Mix with an equal quantity, or a little
more, of good lettuce and dress liberally with a rich mayonnaise dressing made with a glassful of sherry or Maderia
wine, and garnished with olives as in turtle salad. This
salad can also be made with equal quantities of calf's head
and cold boiled vegetables such as potatoes, beets etc., and
dressed with mayonnaise or French dressing. Minced chervil, chives, mint or any other sweet herbs can be sprinkled
over it if a little of this sort of flavoring is relished.

Salad of young Pigs. Lean fresh pork that is tender
and white when roasted is considered better than veal as a
substitute for chicken in salad. It is improved if slightly
corned and the piece known as "spare rib" is best to use.
Roast and put in a cold place for twenty-four hours and
then cut into half inch pieces or a little smaller, rejecting

all brown, fat or tough pieces. Mix with an equal quantity
sliced celery and serve with mayonnaise dressing as with
chicken salad. If preferred the meat of any part of a very
young pig may be cut into half inch pieces and mixed with
equal quantities of sliced celery and fresh crisp acid apples
and mayonnaise dressing. A little sage or sweet marjoram
can be used to flavor the dressing and decorations of sliced
pickled beets or rounds of firm cranberry jelly. Roast apples can be served with it. Do not marinade the meat as
with dry meats.

Sweet-bread Salad. Place the sweet-breads in scalding
salted water for about ten minutes then put in ice water to
whiten them and let remain until thoroughly chilled. Boil
for ten or fifteen minutes and then drain removing any
veins or unsightly portions and put on ice to harden. When
ready cut into pieces of convenient size for eating and arrange in a salad bowl with an equal quantity of crisp lettuce or celery and mayonnaise dressing.

Ham Salad. Take equal quantities of cold boiled ham
cut into dice the size of peas allowing part of the fat to remain, and sliced celery or shredded lettuce. Serve with
boiled dressing or any other kind preferred. See corned
beef salad.

Liver Salad. Baked or broiled lamb's or calf's liver or
what is even more delicate, the boiled liver of fowls, cut
into half inch pieces and sprinkled with salt can be served
with a little more than the same quantity of lettuce or
sliced celery and remoulade dressing. Chopped mustard
leaves or cress can be scattered over it.

Corned Beef Salad. Corned beef for salad must be tender and free from gristle and too much fat. It may be
used in vegetable salads or in place of fresh beef in beef
salads. The old fashioned corned beef salad is made by
cutting the beef into strips about an inch long and a quar-

ter of an inch wide and sprinkling with grated horseradish
or horseradish vinegar. To about one pound of beef add a
large boiled potato and one beet, cut into dice or slices, and
dress the whole with French dressing. Endive is a good
addition. A good modern way is to slice the beef as thin
as possible, using a very sharp thin bladed knife and lay
these curls of meat on leaves of lettuce of about the same
size, and season delicately with any dresssing, mayonnaise
preferred. Chopped cresses or any herb may be used in
place of the other dressings. Roll the leaves of lettuce up
and if necessary tie with a string to keep them in shape.
They are to be taken in the hand and eaten as are sandwiches. They are very decorative piled on a plate or small
platter. Have a firm dressing and do not put on too much.
Cold ham, jerked beef or venison can be used in the same way.

Hamburg Salad.   Divide a plain potato or other vegetable salad, dressed with plenty of French dressing in the
usual way. Put half of the vegetable salad in the bottom
of a salad bowl and on that put half a pound or more according to size salad wished, of tender raw beef that has
been chopped fine and highly seasoned with salt, onion
juice, Cayenne peppe ro rtobasco sauce. Put the rest of the
vegetable salad on the beef and just before serving mix all
together.

Army Salad.   Shred about a quarter of a medium size
head of cabbage and sprinkle well with salt, let it stand
and when the salad is wanted mix with about a pint or a
little more of cold boiled potatoes sliced and sprinkle with a
little vinegar (if a sour dressing is used this may be omitted)
and a pound of cold boiled ham cut into small dice shaped
pieces. Add three or four small pickled onions minced very
fine, and sprinkle lightly with red or black pepper according to taste. Hard boiled eggs may be mixed with it or arranged on top. Mix lightly just before serving, with any
good salad dressing available.

Beef Steak Salad. If you have a good piece of cold broiled steak that is rare and tender cut it into thin slices about three-fourth of an inch long, carefully discarding all hard portions, and mix in a salad bowl with an equal quantity of water or garden cress and French dressing made with few drops of onion juice. The oil may be omitted in whole or in part if the steak was well buttered while hot, as it should have been, and then put in an ice chest to become cold and firm. Lettuce or celery can be added if desired. If the steak is well done or somewhat dry it can be served with potato salad as in roast beef salad using a more liberal quantity of dressing than is required with green herbs. Green peas are an addition to this salad that is much liked. It is always better to have the steak well buttered and seasoned with salt and pepper while still hot and then put in a cold place to harden. Cold French fried potatoes or chips are good to serve with it if potatoes do not form a part of the salad. This is a good supper salad for hot weather.

Turtle Salad. Cold boiled turtle or turtle stock make a rich salad which should not be served, however, with a meal in which turtle is served in other ways. Have equal quantities of the different kinds of meat cut into half inch pieces. Salt the meat well and sprinkle with lemon juice if it is dry and serve with plenty of crisp lettuce, shredded olives and a rich mayonnaise dressing made with turtle eggs, if you have them, adding a wineglassful of sherry wine or Maderia. The wine may be sprinkled over the meat, unless the dressing is thick and requires thinning. The turtle eggs should be well boiled but, as they will not turn hard, only the yolks had best be used. Hard boiled fowl's eggs or those of wild birds can be used to decorate the salad. Pickled limes are good to serve with this salad.

Rabbit Salad. The meat of wild or tame rabbits can be used. Cut the meat of two roasted rabbits into one-half inch pieces, cool with a plain dressing and let it stand for several hours. A few slices of onion, bruised leaves of thyme, tarragon, tender buds of black birch or any field herb to give a wild flavor, can be added. When ready for the salad, remove the herbs etc., carefully from the meat, mix in a bowl with the heads of lettuce torn into small pieces and serve with mayonnaise dressing into which a large teaspoonful of prepared French mustard has been well beaten. Water cresses are a nice garnish.

Venison Salad. Venison is too dry to make a really fine salad but cold venison is good served with potato salad in any of the ways cold beef is relished. Take a pound of cold venison and cut into half inch cubes. Pour over it a French dressing and let it stand for an hour or two and then mix with lettuce or endive, the latter preferred. A few cresses, dandelions, chives or any slightly bitter herbs that are relished, can be added. Put on more dressing, if too dry, and serve.

Vegetable Salads.

THE opportunity for making delicious salads is greater with vegetables than with any other article of food used on American tables. There is scarcely a vegetable in common use but what may be made into various delicious salads with the addition of a few inexpensive condiments, thus varying the menu of vegetables to a degree possible in no other way.

LETTUCE SALADS.

Lettuce is the most universal and popular of all salads either by itself or used as the foundation for many other salads. Its mild flavor combines well with all seasonings. Lettuce should be torn or broken if necessary to make the leaves smaller, as cutting wilts it, excepting, of course, when shredded lettuce is wanted. It should be gathered early in the morning before the sun is hot and kept in a cold tight place where there is little evaporation. Wrapping the heads in paper tends to preserve them. The stems can be placed in water but do not soak the whole head as that makes it flabby. If necessary to wash it do so quickly and shake all the water off. Never let the lettuce soak in the dressing or it will become wilted and tough.

Plain Lettuce Salads. Dress clean crisp lettuce with French dressing. For convenience the dressing is often put upon the lettuce unmixed. Mix a tablespoonful of oil with a saltspoonful of salt and scatter over the lettuce: pour over three more tablespoonfuls of oil and toss about until every part of the lettuce is covered with oil, then add a tablespoonful of good vinegar and mix gently scattering a salt-

73

spoonful of fresh pepper evenly over it. Eat at once. The amount of dressing will, of course, be in proportion to the amount of lettuce but these proportions, three-fourths oil to one-fourth vinegar, will meet general requirements. When lettuce first comes on the market in the spring the primitive way of eating it with a little salt only is considered preferable by many. Adding a little oil to the salt improves it very much and in this way is often quite as satisfactory as when made with great elaboration. Sugar and vinegar is still the favorite dressing with many people and although condemed as vulgar because of being a general practice, it is a wholesome and convenient way of dressing lettuce. Lemon juice and water with sugar is another favorite dressing.

The varieties of lettuce are numerous and more to be considered from the gardener's point of view than the salad maker's, as for his or her use the Romaine or Cos varieties are best for lettuce salads and the cabbage sorts for mixing with meat or lobster.

Salad of Romaine Lettuce. To accompany game or Guinea fowls. Take one large or two small heads and avoid washing or wetting if it is possible. Reject all wilted or defective leaves and cut off the green ends leaving only the white crisp leaves and stalks. Put in a cool dry salad bowl and dress with a plain dressing. Sprinkle finely minced tarragon leaves evenly through it after it is well covered with the dressing.

French Lettuce Salads. These are made with French dressing sprinkled with chopped herbs, chervil, chives, sliced radishes, chicory leaves, tarragon, parsley, mint, etc., being used. The salad bowl is usually rubbed with onion or garlic or a "chapon" is used. When fresh herbs are not to be had, herb vinegar may be substituted.

Salad of Lettuce Stalks. When the lettuce in the garden shoots up quickly during the summer into long seed stalks it can be utilized by stripping the stalks of leaves, cutting the tender portions into lengths and tieing in bundles like asparagus. Boil until tender and when cold and well drained serve with mayonnaise, French dressing or sauce piquant.

Cress Salad. Water cresses and the common garden cress, pepper-grass etc., are most wholesome and popular but the abomniable habit in most restaurants of garnishing every dish with water cress is, to say the least, tiresome. They may be properly used in moderation to accompany boiled meats and cold roast meats. The young fresh leaves are tender and mild and these only should be used for salad for the older leaves are too strong, tough and bitter. Dress with French dressing which by many is preferred with the oil omitted. Equal parts of sliced celery and cresses are good so are one-third cresses and two-thirds cucumbers using French or mayonnaise dressing. Chopped cresses are an agreeable addition to many green salads such as chicory and lettuce. Cress to be eaten with steak or cold meat is best prepared by washing quickly in cold salted vinegar and water and serving at once. Water cresses and thin sliced crisp apple are delicious made with French dressing and served with water fowl. Have the cress dry and crisp and the salad cold.

Endive or Escarole Salad. This is one of the best of green salads and makes a welcome change from lettuce late in the season. It should be well blanched and crisp as only the white leaves are to be eaten. Serve the same as lettuce with French dressing. Chopped chives or at least a suspicion of onion or garlic is thought indispensable by the French. A "chapon" is often used in mixing it. There are numerous varieties of endive, and all are good for salad purposes. Chopped chervil and tarragon among herbs are preferred to sprinkle over the salad.

Chicory and Doucette. These are of the same nature as

endive and in salad mixing should be treated in the same way. Do not put on the dressing until ready to serve.

Dandelion Salads. These are not yet popular in the United States but the peculiar bitterness is relished by some people and is said to be most healthful. The blanched leaves only are fit for salad, tied up and treated as with endive. Wash carefully and serve with French dressing.

Dandelion with Beet. Mix a pint of white dandelion leaves with two fair sized boiled beets sliced small and served with French dressing.

Dandelion a la Contoise is dandelion served with bacon dressing.

Celery Salads. Celery is the most popular and abundant of winter salads with us and is nowhere found in such perfection as in the United States. Its own delicious flavor and crispness are most welcome with no dressing except a little fine salt. Exercise care to see that the celery is clean and fresh and no way of serving it will be more liked than this. Do not crowd the stalks into a celery glass or goblet but serve on a flat dish. Split the heads into convenient sized pieces and let it come to the table cold and dry.

Plain Celery Salad. Cut clean crisp stalks of celery into pieces not quite an inch in length, unless the stalks are small, and serve with mayonnaise dressing without letting the dressing remain on it long. French dressing is not considered as good. Always have the salad cold. The celery can be cut into narrow straws and these curled by putting them into ice water. They should be two or three inches long. This salad does not require garnishing but the leaves of the white plumed kinds are attractive when arranged around the dish.

Celery and Apple Salad. Have three cups of sliced celery to two of sliced or chopped acid apple. Mix with mayonnaise and serve at once after cutting the apples.

Celery and Radish Salad. Three-fourth shredded celery and one-fourth radishes sliced very thin. Dress with may-onnaise. Cover the top with part of the sliced radishes.

Celery and Walnut Salad. Have crisp celery cut into small pieces with one-third the quantity of the meat of English walnuts broken in halves, and the whole well dressed with mayonnaise and garnished with lettuce or cresses.

Waldorf Salad. Pare, core and cut into small squares four large tart apples, add to them a quart of celery that has been cut into half inch pieces and sprinkle over all a teaspoonful of salt, one of paprika and two of tarragon vine-gar. Mix together with a teacup and a half full of good stiff mayonnaise dressing. Serve on lettuce leaves.

Spinach Salad. Spinach is not so much used as formerly for green salads other things having taken its place, but it will be found useful to increase the quantity of other green salads or served by itself. Gather a quart of the small freshly grown leaves from the centres of the plants and serve with a French dressing. A little onion, a few sorrel leaves and chopped mint or chervil will be pleasing additions.

Cabbage Salads. These are among the oldest forms of salad known and although pretentious people affect to despise them, sliced cabbage is commonly found on the most elegant and well appointed tables. Raw cabbage is more healthful than cooked cabbage. There is a great difference in the flavor of cabbages and for salads, care should be taken to choose those that are firm and solid with a sweet " nutty " flavor. Red cabbage is preferred by the Germans but Americans like the appearance of the white varieties best. However, a little of the red arranged on the border or mixed with the white gives a pleasing effect. Cabbage is mixed with all kinds of winter salads in Europe and by the foreign population of this country, but is more satisfactory to American palates dressed by itself in various ways. As a rule cabbage salad requires more salt than most other kinds.

Plain Cabbage Salads. Shred as much delicate finely flavored cabbage as is wanted and dress it with the best of olive oil and a little fine salt only, tossing it about until every part is covered with a delicate coating of oil. As an accompaniment to oysters nothing better is likely to be wanted. French dressing may be used in place of the oil and salt if desired.

Plain Cold Slaw. Slice as much good cabbage as is wanted and sprinkle with salt, pepper and a little sugar: toss about with a salad fork until the condiments are evenly distributed and then sprinkle with good vinegar and toss again. This is usually served on little plates, or piled in the centre of a platter surrounded by fried oysters some of each going to each guest.

Cold Slaw. Shred as much sweet white cabbage as is wanted or chop it if preferred, scatter a little fine salt all through it and mix it with a dressing made of two well-beaten eggs, a piece of butter half the size of an egg, a teaspoonful of made mustard, two tablespoonfuls of fine sugar and a teacupful of vinegar. Cook in a double boiler or in a bowl in the top of a kettle until it becomes like a soft custard. When cold half a teacupful of cream can be added but it is good without it. Pour over the cabbage. Mix well and put in a cold place until ready to serve.

Cabbage with Celery. Fine white cabbage sliced thin with celery in equal quantities and served with mayonnaise or French dressing, is thought by some to be an improvement over plain celery.

Cabbage and Celery Salad. Two-thirds cabbage chopped or shredded fine and one-third celery cut fine. Salt the cabbage and mix with olive oil until all is covered with a slight coating of oil. Make a dressing of three eggs well beaten, one scant teaspoonful of mustard and the same of salt, a large teaspoonful of butter, one teaspoonful of sugar and one-half cup of vinegar. Mix dressing well together and heat carefully in a double boiler or over a boiling kettle stirring all the time and adding pepper to taste. When it boils or thickens throw over the cabbage and celery and mix all together.

Cabbage and Veal Salad. Have equal quantities of sliced white cabbage and cold roast veal free from gristle or brown parts and dress with mayonnaise, or better still with the following. One teaspoonful prepared mustard, one of salt and one of sugar. Mix well in a cupful of warm water and stir in two well-beaten eggs then add one-half cupful of oil, melted butter or sweet cream. Cook in a double boiler or over hot water until it begins to thicken then take from the fire and stir in slowly one-half cupful of vinegar.

Cabbage with Bacon Dressing. Shred as much cabbage as wanted, soak for half an hour in cold water with a little salt, drain dry and pour over it a bacon dressing. Hard boiled eggs and slices of beet are usually served as garnishings.

Hot Slaw. Cover shredded cabbage in a sauce-pan with salted water, and boil until tender but not until it loses shape. Drain in a warm place and pour over it a hot Bernaise sauce. Good with steaks, chops, fritters etc.

Cabbage Salad or Hot Slaw. Have a small head of cabbage or half a large one, finely shredded. Heat separately a cupful of sweet milk and half a cupful of vinegar. When the vinegar is hot stir into it a tablespoonful of white sugar and one of butter, a teaspoonful of salt and one of celery essence if liked, and a quarter of a teaspoonful of pepper, Cayenne preferred. Pour over the cabbage and let all get hot but do not cook long enough to make the cabbage flabby, then turn into a bowl and pour over it the hot

milk, into which has been previously stirred two well beaten
eggs until it begins to harden. Mix well and quickly with
a wooden or silver salad fork, cover and place where it will
cool quickly and not lose its crispness.

Salad of Cabbage Sprouts. The tender sprouts that first
start from the stump of winter cabbages when planted out
in the spring or under glass, makes a most refreshing spring
salad when other salad material is scarce. Gather them
when very young and tender and dress with any salad
dressing liked. Young mustard leaves, chives, rareripes
or any spring salad herbs can be dressed with them.

Cabbage Palm Salad. The centre of the heads of many
of the sabal and areca palms make a very good salad, but
as a whole tree has to be destroyed to furnish a small edible
portion it is to be hoped the use of this salad will not become general. Cut the tender white hearts into shreds and
serve with French dressing. Sprinkle with any minced salad
herbs whose flavor is liked. If it is bitter it can be improved by soaking half an hour in salted water before dressing. A bacon sauce can be used in camp where others are
not to be had.

Salad of Beet Leaves. The seed leaves of beets that are
thinned out of the rows in early spring make an excellent
salad if used before they become tough. Later in the season while the beets are still growing, cut as many as are
wanted of the small leaves just unfolding from the centre of
the plant, and serve alone or with other things in any of
the ways in which lettuce is served. Gather the centre
leaves early in the morning before the sun has wilted them
using either garden or field beets.

Salad of Swiss Chard. Chard is a variety of beet having large succulent stalks to the leaves. These stalks should
be cut before they are old and tough, tied in a bundle like

asparagus and trimmed in equal lengths. Boil in salted water until tender, drain and serve cold with French dressing or piquant sauce as with asparagus.

Salad of Turnip Tops. It is well to know that the blanched sprouts of the large French or Russian turnips make one of the finest of winter salads. They can be raised early in any warm dark cellar in great abundance but I would not advise their cultivation under dwelling houses. The quicker the growth of the plants the more crisp and delicate they are. Pick them when three or four inches long and serve with French dressing. They are improved by scalding in hot water for a moment, plunged in ice water then drained and dressed as before.

English Spring Salad. The English spring salad that is so often spoken of is only the early cress and young seed-leaf mustard mixed with radishes, young onions, small lettuce or any early salad plants in season using. French or plain dressing.

Pepper Salads. The use of green or uncooked peppers is becoming more general each year as their delightful qualities are better known and new ways of serving them are discovered. Their healthfulness is acknowledged by all and when once their use becomes familiar, a dinner is considered incomplete without them in some form. Our warm summers, even in the northern part of the country, enable us to grow peppers in our salad gardens and to enjoy this tropical treat as our European friends can never hope to. There are a great number of varieties of peppers, some of them as mild as lettuce, others so strong as to be almost blinding to look at. Most of the strong and fiery qualities of a pepper are in the seeds and veins so that by removing these parts almost any pepper can be made edible. Peppers are always peeled by those who understand best how to use them. Peeling improves their flavor wonderfully and with a little practice the work is easily done, a small sharp and pointed knife being the only tool necessary.

Mexican " Snow " Salad. Take twelve large sweet peppers wipe them carefully and broil over a slow fire only long enough to blister their skins. Then carefully peel off the outer skin, split them open with a sharp knife, take out the core, seed and fleshy veins, without breaking the outer walls of the pepper, wash in salted water, dry and fill with sardines mixed with lime or lemon juice and mashed with a fork after the skin and bones have been removed. Oysters, chicken or any delicate meat carefully seasoned may be substituted for the sardines. Put a little of the filling in each pepper and arrange them on a platter or flat salad dish and pour a French dressing over them. Have ready a " snow," made by taking the meat from a hundred English walnuts and soaking in water half an hour to loosen the dark skin which must be carefully removed or it will give a gray color to the snow. Grind the meat very fine in a stone or porcelain lined mortar adding a little sweet milk to moisten it, then with a fork beat it up very light adding powdered sugar to taste. In Mexico it is made quite sweet. Sprinkle this over the peppers making it look as much like snow as possible and on top strew half a cupful of crimson pomegranate grains. Of course this last will have to be omitted when pomegranates cannot be obtained but it adds greatly to the appearance of the dish.

Mexican Pepper Salad. Broil and peel twelve large sweet peppers as directed in the preceding recipe : cut them into narrow strips lengthwise and lay them on slices of raw tomatoes. Cut two rarepipes very thin (or use a few drops of onion juice) mix with salt, oil and vinegar as in French dressing, and add a little sage, powdering it if dry or if green have it crushed in the oil some time before using and then remove. This salad is very delicate when eaten with fresh cream cheese.

Andalusian Salad (*Gaspacho.*) This is a favorite with Spanish peasants and is made by putting a layer of stale bread, cut in small slices, in the bottom of a bowl and sprinkling plentifully with oil and a little vinegar and then slicing Spanish or other mild onions over it with tomatoes and green cucumbers all delicately sliced and sprinkled with salt and red pepper. Then add more bread and plenty of oil with the various vegetables named until the quantity is sufficient. Let it stand for an hour or two in a cool place and scatter a large handful of bread crumbs on top when ready to serve. If too dry moisten with more oil or ice water.

Pepper Baskets. Peel carefully large sweet bell, or Spanish peppers, removing the seed and core. Fill with sardine or any good fish salad, chopped chicken with mayonnaise, shrimp, lobster or any similar thing preferred. Stuff with cucumber to serve with fish. Have very cold with French dressing.

Lamb's Lettuce, Corn Salad, Fetticos, Winter Salad etc., are all names of the same plants differing occasionally in small particulars of growth in different localities but practically the same in salad making. Valuable for use in the winter months. Dress with French dressing in the same manner as lettuce and use to accompany roast meats, salted fish etc. The mild flavor combines well with celery, cresses, chives or other herbs.

Turnip Salad. It takes a Col. Sellers to serve a plain turnip salad and I do not recommend it unless under stress of circumstances. Cold boiled turnips will be found a welcome addition to nearly all mixed vegetables, and Macedoine salads, while small, young, tender turnips raw are good sliced very thin in a mixed green salad with a French dressing.

Sorrel Salad. The cultivated sorrel is one of the most generally employed herbs in France but is not yet popular here. It is an agreeable and wholesome addition to any green salad. The wild variety is just as good but smaller and the young and tender leaves of the wild oxalis are good sprinkled in salads. Use less vinegar when either sorrel or oxalis are used. Select only the young and tender leaves and tear them apart if necessary to make them smaller.

Radishes in Salads. No. 1. The use of radishes is so familiar to all that no directions are required. Those who like them agree that any other addition than a little salt is superfluous. The small radishes are the most attractive for a garnish with green salads, and thinly sliced they can be introduced with almost any green salad. For a salad of radishes scrape the red skin from some of the long varieties and cut them into strips using French dressing.

Radish Salad No. 2. Take long red radishes when fresh and crisp and carefully scrape off nearly or quite all of the outside red skin or the salad will be too pungent. Then with a wooden pestle crush the radishes by laying on a table and striking on the sides until they are broken enough for the dressing to penetrate readily. Arrange on a bed of lettuce leaves like the spokes of a wheel, or build a three or four sided pyramid by placing them as a log or cob house is built. Cover with French dressing and sprinkle with finely minced chives. This is an old fashioned French recipe known to have been in use over seventy-five years.

Radish Salad No. 3. Another radish salad but little known is made by cutting the radishes into very thin slices and soaking them in cold salted water to flavor and render them mild. When the salad is wanted dress with a French dressing made with onion juice, or mix with chopped chives or very tender spring onions delicately sliced. This is good to serve with fish in place of cucumbers.

Radish Salad No. 4. Waldorf. This is served with meat pies or hot meats. Four large tart apples are pared, cut into small pieces and mixed immediately with a teaspoonful of salt, one of paprika and two tablespoonfuls of tarragon vinegar. Pour over the whole a large cupful of mayonnaise dressing. Serve on leaves of lettuce.

Radish Leaf Salad. When the rows of young radishes are being thinned a very good salad can be made from the leaves of those taken out. Serve with French dressing made with a little onion juice, or sprinkled with minced chives. Excellent in potato salads.

Parsnip Salad. A parsnip salad is most welcome in the North during the spring before fresh vegetables can be obtained. Slice cold boiled parsnips, those which have been in the open ground all winter being best, and dress with mayonnaise or French dressing. A few green leaves of cresses or radishes will add to the flavor.

Salad of Salsify or Oyster Plant. Cut the boiled roots into little round slices crosswise and while still hot pour over them a little Rhine or other white wine and allow to get cold. They can then be served alone with French dressing or mixed with endive, chopped beet and potato.

Kohl-Rabi Salad. The turnip rooted cabbage is boiled and used in salads in the same way as potatoes, carrots etc.

Mexican Rare-ripe Salad. Boil a dozen large rare-ripes (not onions as a rule, though mild or Spanish onions may be used in this way) in salted water until tender but do not allow them to break apart. When cold, open carefully with a knife and fold back the leaves. Put each one in a nest of lettuce leaves and then put in the centre of the rare-ripe a teaspoonful of mayonnaise dressing. This delicious salad does not leave the unpleasant after-effects of raw rare-ripes.

Mixed Summer Salad. Almost any combination of green herbs, blending the mild and strong together in agreeable proportions, treated with a good dressing and served cold and crisp will be enjoyed. Try two or three heads of lettuce, according to size, a small handful of green mustard leaves and one of water cress, five tender radishes and one cucumber sliced thin. Make a dressing of two teaspoonfuls of white sugar, one of salt a little pepper and six table-spoonfuls of vinegar. Two or three times as much oil is often added but generally a salad of mustard or cress is preferred without oil. Foreigners like cheese and bread and butter with green salads.

TOMATO SALADS.

Salads of tomatoes are almost endless in variety being served with almost any salad materials. Some of these combinations are the most delicious among salads, but it is a mistake to put tomatoes in every thing simply because they are well liked.

Plain Tomato Salad. This salad is acceptable to almost every one with roasted or broiled meats. Always peel the tomatoes if possible. If the tomatoes are smooth and fair the work is easily done with a small bladed sharp knife and is still easier if they are scalded for a moment by pouring boiling hot water over them which enables one to easily remove the skin. A still better way is to place them in a wire basket and plunge in boiling water for a moment. After peeling, put the tomatoes on ice and when cold serve. It increases the apparent quantity to slice them but when we have smooth medium sized tomatoes, solid to the core, they are most elegant served whole with a spoonful of mayonnaise or French dressing. A red tomato on a pale leaf of lettuce looks very appetizing and is a good way in which to serve them.

Simple Tomato Salads. A salad greatly relished by many children, and older people as well, is of sliced tomatoes sprinkled liberally with sugar and a few drops of vinegar. Tomatoes with sugar and cream are good for supper or tea if the cream is the real article for milk will not answer as a substitute. Give the tomatoes a very slight sprinkling of salt before placing on the table but put the cream on, at the table, just before eating.

Tomato and Lettuce Salad. This is extremely dainty, and a good way to serve the combination, when the proportions of tomatoes are limited, is to arrange the lettuce prettily in a bowl or on a platter and put the tomatoes on the lettuce after they have been peeled and cut into convenient size pieces for eating. Just before serving dress with mayonnaise or French dressing, or put some of the salad on a plate and pour a ladleful of dressing over it before serving each guest.

Variations of these plain tomato salads are made by sprinkling them with chopped green herbs, chives, tarragon, parsley, coriander, chicory, cress, dandelion, pepper, sage or mint. Perhaps chives and tarragon are the most desirable although the others are good. Do not use them so plentifully as to destroy the taste of the tomato. Flavored vinegar can be used when the green herbs are not to be had and a French dressing is preferable to a mayonnaise for use with them.

Tomato Salad with Cheese. Arrange the tomatoes, peeled and sliced in a salad bowl, in layers, sprinkling a liberal quantity of grated Parmesan cheese over each layer. Make a dressing, allowing for two fair sized tomatoes one tablespoonful of oil, two of Rhine wine, a saltspoonful of salt and pepper. Mix and serve cold, sprinkling a little grated cheese over the top.

Stuffed Tomatoes or Tomato Baskets, as they are called are attractive served as tomato salads and as they can be prepared before hand and arranged on separate plates in the pantry, they are conveniently served to large companies. Place a fresh crisp green leaf of lettuce on each plate and put the tomato on that. Choose as far as possible, smooth, medium sized ripe tomatoes and peel, cutting a small piece from the stem end removing the core and as many of the seeds as desired. Fill with any of the following mixtures and put on ice. When about to serve put a spoonful of mayonnaise dressing over each one, or better still pass the dressing in a pretty bowl and let the guest help themselves. These are the various mixtures which may be used.

Sweetbreads boiled, cut into small pieces and mixed with the meat of nuts.

Hard boiled eggs mixed with lettuce or endive cut fine

Celery cut fine and mixed with mayonnaise.

Celery and chicken, or veal, seasoned to taste.

Cold boiled green peas.

Tender string beans cut into small pieces and mixed with French dressing.

Fresh cucumbers cut thin with, or without onions.

Shrimp cut up and mixed with mayonnaise.

Lobster and crab meat cut fine and mixed with mayonnaise.

Boiled beef tongue chopped and seasoned.

Chopped cresses and shaved dried or jerked beef.

Salad a la Muellaire. Peel round, even sized tomatoes, cut out the inside quite deep. Take cucumbers after soaking well in cold water, pare and cut into dice, add about an equal quantity of the inside of the tomato, season with salt, vinegar, oil and chopped parsley. Mix well and fill the tomatoes. Have them cold and when ready to serve put on mayonnaise dressing and garnish with lettuce.

Spiced Tomato Salad. Tomatoes are delicious to many served by removing the inside and mixing with equal parts of brown sugar and dry mustard, a little salt, pepper sauce or plain vinegar according to taste. The seeds, if numerous, can be removed by passing the pulp through a sieve. Stir the mixture into a paste and refill the tomatoes.

Tomato Salad with Cream. Rub the salad bowl with garlic and slice fine, ripe peeled tomatoes into the bowl: sprinkle with salt and paprika and let them stand in the ice chest until very cold and ready to serve. Drain the water from the tomatoes and pour over them rich whipped cream, or pass the cream to each guest. This is an excellent salad to serve with fried or broiled chicken as a change from the usual tomato and mayonnaise.

Tomato and Beef Salad. Cut into slices or convenient sized pieces for eating, cold boiled or braised beef. Let the beef marinate or soak in oil or vinegar, seasoned with salt and pepper. When wanted arrange in a salad bowl with cold, peeled ripe tomatoes (about one-quarter more tomato than beef) sliced or cut into pieces. Sprinkle, as you put the layers in, with finely cut up chives and chervil and serve with French dressing.

Yellow Tomatoes are excellent for salads although not popular. They may be used in any of the ways in which red ones are used and furnish a pleasing variety. When red cooked tomatoes have been served at a dinner it seems less like the same thing to have a salad of yellow tomatoes. The small yellow egg tomatoes make an attractive salad served whole, and look like plums in a fruit or sweet salad. Remove the skins carefully and when they are very cold pile on a dish like fruit. They make a good garnish for a red tomato salad. Cream also harmonizes well in flavor with yellow tomatoes.

Tomato and Cress Salad. Take four to six ripe red tomatoes and after peeling, slice and while doing so remove and save the seeds and soft pulp surrounding them. Pass this pulp through a fine sieve to remove the seeds, and make a dressing by mixing with it the yolks of two hard boiled eggs, a saltspoonful of salt, one of pepper and a teaspoonful of made mustard, if mustard is liked. Pick over and clean carefully the watercress and dip in salted vinegar, and arrange in the centre of a dish with the tomato rings

around them. Have about equal quantities of tomatoes and
cress. When ready to serve pour the dressing over and
mix. Lettuce is often added and if the cresses are strong
is an improvement. Mayonnaise dressing is sometimes added when serving.

Salad a la May Irwin. Six medium sized tomatoes cut
in quarters, two or three cucumbers cut in thick slices, one
Spanish onion, three green peppers and two large sour apples are chopped up together. Make a dressing with twice
the amount of oil used to the red wine vinegar, half a teaspoonful of mustard, one of Worcestershire sauce, one of
brown sugar, one or more of salt, half a one of red pepper.
Mix all well together in a dish or bowl rubbed with a
crushed clove or garlic, turn into an ornamented salad bowl
and put on ice. Serve with it Roquefort cheese and guava
jelly.

Cucumber Salads. The sooner cucumbers are served
after being picked from the vines the more crisp and healthful they are. If they must be kept some time before serving, put the stem end in water or throw the whole vegetable
into ice water. Do not slice them into water as that makes
them tough and indigestible. Place the cucumber on ice
before preparing. Cut off the bitter ends and slice very
thinly with a sharp knife and serve with a French dressing.
If a little onion flavor is wanted add a few drops of onion
juice to the dressing, or rub the dish with garlic before
mixing the salad. If a cucumber and onion salad is wanted
slice fresh young onions very thin with an equal quantity
of thin sliced cucumbers and dress with salt, pepper, vinegar and oil. The oil may be omitted if the taste is not relished. Chives cut fine are also good with cucumbers while
cress and cucumbers make a good combination.

Cucumber and Pepper Salad. Peel and remove the seeds
from two sweet Spanish peppers, shave into slivers and mix
with two medium sized cucumbers peeled, cut into thin

slices, and sprinkled with salt. A few minced chives or tarragon leaves are an improvement. Use a French dressing to which mustard can be added if wanted.

Cucumber Boats or stuffed cucumbers are made by peeling the cucumbers and cutting them in two lengthwise and then scraping out the seeds. Put the pieces on ice and when the salad is wanted fill with any good salad mixture and mayonnaise dressing. A good filling is made with chopped tomatoes, celery, a few drops of onion juice and mayonnaise dressing. Medium sized cucumbers are best to use. Arrange on lettuce leaves and if the cucumbers are large, the pieces may be cut in two when served. Thin slices of radishes with the red skin left on makes a pretty garnish.

Cucumber and Tomato Salad. Peel and slice cucumbers and tomatoes and arrange in alternate layers. Use French or mayonnaise dressing as preferred. In serving to a number of guests both dressings may be had and passed to the guests for their preference.

Cucumbers with Fish. A change from the usual arrangement of sliced cucumbers when served as an accompaniment to fish, is to cut them in two lengthwise, and then, placing them flat side down on a dish, cut into thin slices without destroying the shape. Serve with French dressing.

Crummock or Skirret Salad. Skirret is a vegetable root not much grown in this country: it resembles a small divided parsnip in appearance and flavor, but is considered more delicate for salads. Serve with French dressing as in boiled parsnip salad, or boil and when cold slice and mix with equal quantities of cold boiled potatoes and crisp celery and mayonnaise dressing.

Pickled Walnut Salad. Put a layer of cold boiled potatoes sliced in a salad bowl and season with salt and pepper. On these place a layer of pickled walnuts sliced as thinly

Borecole Salad. This vegetable, better known under the name of Kale, is much used by foreigners who make a salad of it by selecting the young tender leaves and mix with about one-third the quantity of young sorrel leaves, chives chopped or any other herb liked. Serve with French dressing. This salad is nice with head cheese, cold ham or hard boiled eggs.

Asparagus Salad. Opinions differ as to which is best the blanched or green asparagus but both are good for salad making if they are fresh. No asparagus is equal to that freshly cut from the garden, boiled early in the morning and put on ice until wanted. Scrape and clean the stalks and tie in convenient bundles: if not ready to boil stand them in cold water. When ready stand in salted water having the water come just below the heads which will prevent them boiling to pieces: then steam in a covered kettle cooking the tender parts while the stem ends are boiling. Boil until tender, fifteen minutes to a half hour according to age. Drain and put on ice. When wanted arrange prettily on a flat dish with the heads all one way and serve with separate plates of French dressing or vinaigrette sauce into which each stalk can be dipped before it is eaten. This is good by itself or with any cold meat, especially lamb or chicken.

Asparagus a la Vinaigrette. Boil the asparagus until tender but not longer or it will injure the flavor. Have ready a French dressing made with plenty of onion juice, a little extra pepper and a teaspoonful of French mustard. Pour over the asparagus while hot, cover and cool. Keep on ice and when ready to serve drain from the dressing and arrange on a flat dish. A little Remoulade sauce can be served with it if anything additional is wanted.

Salad of Asparagus Tips. Often when the stalks are too old for use there are plenty of green tips to the asparagus which are available for a most delicious salad. Boil in a little salted water until tender and then drain. An onion sliced in the water helps the flavor. When cold arrange in a salad bowl with torn lettuce and serve with French dressing or mayonnaise dressing. New potatoes or cauliflower in about equal proportions are good to mix with the asparagus in salad. Hard boiled eggs and capers are good garnishes.

Asparagus Salad with Cray-fish. Cut the tender parts of cold boiled asparagus into pieces of equal size and mix with about one-third the quantity of pared crayfish tails, seasoning with salt and a very little Cayenne pepper. Make a dressing by rubbing to a cream the yolks of six hard boiled eggs with a little oil, and then thinning with vinegar and pouring over the asparagus and crayfish.

Salad of French Artichokes. The French artichoke is easily raised in many sections of our country and its delicate flavor is much appreciated by those who have acquired a taste for them but they have never become popular. Most of these found in the northern markets are brought from France and command fancy prices, although not so delicate in flavor as those grown in the southern sections of our own country. Pare off the stems, trim away the coarse lower leaves and boil in salted water from twenty to thirty-five minutes or until the bottoms are tender. Frenchmen love to pull them to pieces while hot, dipping the pieces into dressing and eating them at once, but I fancy Americans will like them better if prepared by letting them cool and then removing the choke, and cutting the bottom or edible portion into strips, also removing the tender white lower tips of the bud leaves and putting them into the salad bowl with a head of bleached chicory, endive or lettuce and mixed with a French dressing. Allow four artichoke globes to one head of chicory. Cold boiled tongue or ham is sometimes mixed with the salad. Frequently the boiled flower buds are cut in two and the dressing is poured over them, but it is an awkward thing to separate the hard and edible portions at the table. The tender bottoms of the young artichoke flowers are made into a salad by cutting into thin strips when raw mixing with sliced cucumbers, three artichokes to one cucumber, and dressing with French dressing made with onion juice. Place the boiled artichokes upside down to drain.

Jerusalem Artichoke Salad. Wash and scrape the artichoke tubers and boil for twenty minutes: slice and while hot pour over them a French dressing made with onion juice. When cold mix with an equal quantity of good lettuce, add more dressing if the first is all absorbed, any minced flavoring herbs you like, and serve.

STRING BEAN SALADS.

Salads from string beans if well made are most delicious; but if the beans are tough, stringy or stale the result will be an abomination. The several ways of preparing salads from string beans, here given, are recognized as superior to other methods.

Number 1. String the beans and boil several hours in salted water, drain, cool and put on ice. Arrange on a dish in a pile with the ends all the same way and serve with French or mayonnaise dressing. Do not break the beans but keep them whole if possible. A pinch of cooking soda thrown into the water will keep the beans the green color.

Number 2. String a quart of beans, boil until tender in salted water with a large onion sliced and a bunch of parsley, drain and cool. Serve very cold with French dressing and any minced salad herb sprinkled on top.

Number 3. Boil a quart of string beans in salted water until tender, cool and cut into pieces about an inch long.

Put in a salad bowl with a tablespoonful of minced parsley, six shredded olives and two teaspoonfuls of tomato catsup. Serve with French dressing.

Number 4. Cut the beans into four pieces, put in a sauce pan with cold water and when they come to a hard boil the beans will be cooked if young and tender as they should be. An onion may be sliced and boiled with them and then arranged on a dish and served with the beans.

Number 5. Take equal quantities of cold boiled potatoes cut into small pieces, string beans and fresh endive. Rub the bottom of a salad bowl with garlic or half a raw onion and mix with a French dressing. Chopped chervil or other salad herbs will be an improvement.

Number 6. White wax beans make a pretty salad and can be arranged to contrast with the green beans, or one can be used to garnish the other. Boil until tender, carefully remove any dark or discolored portions and serve with white mayonnaise dressing.

Number 7. With a sharp knife shred the string beans into narrow strawlike pieces, either before or after boiling, and then dress in any of the ways mentioned above. The shredded beans can be dressed with a French dressing sometime before using and used to garnish any other salad served with mayonnaise dressing. Or, string the beans and then boil them whole and, when tender and cold, slice them lengthwise cutting each into four long pieces and then serve by themselves or mix in other salads. A small pile of the shredded beans look well arranged on a leaf of lettuce.

Number 8. Boil string beans until very tender, drain and while hot dress with onion juice, vinegar, pepper and salt. When cold add oil or melted butter, carefully tossing them about so a little oil will cover each portion without the beans being broken.

Salad of String Peas. Pea pods can be boiled and served in any of the ways string beans are served. Take perfectly tender, young pea pods about an inch long, and serve with French dressing. Cresses or chervil are good to mix with them as are also sliced tomatoes.

POTATO SALADS.

Potato salads are considered native to the Fatherland and have long been a favorite dish in the various forms served. A generation ago cold potatoes were considered unwholesome in this country but now cold potato salad is common in all sections, while the hot salads of potatoes are not popular. New potatoes are by far the best to use and the salad is best in early summer when such potatoes are in perfecttion. Mealy potatoes are not good in salads. In Germany, special varieties are raised for their good qualities in salad making. The potatoes are considered best if boiled in their skins, peeled and sliced while hot, although it is doubtful if it makes any difference about slicing them hot or cold. Some salad makers insist that the dressing used shall be poured over the potatoes while they are hot, but popular taste is satisfied if they are allowed to cool first. The best and most popular way is to cut the potatoes into slices a quarter or three-eights of an inch thick: if cut too thin the pieces break and do not look attractive. When cut into balls with a potato scoop they are most inviting and when served as an accompaniment to some other dish, on a leaf of lettuce, they are especially attractive. Potatoes absorb a great quantity of dressing and usually a larger proportion of vinegar is acceptable than with green salads. All potato salads can stand for some time after being mixed, without injury.

Plain Potato Salad. This is the usual popular potato salad and is good with any cold meat or sandwiches at any season of the year. Slice cold boiled potatoes into a bowl in layers with onions sliced very thin, or minced very fine, allowing one onion to six or eight potatoes. Dress with a liberal quantity of French dressing. This salad is more delicate if onion juice is used instead of the minced onion in somewhat more liberal quantity than with a green salad. Sprinkle with chopped chervil, tarragon, parsley etc.

Potato Salad a la Philadelphia. Spread slices of cold boiled potato on a flat dish and sprinkle them with vinegar and salt: pour over them a mayonnaise dressing and spot the dressing with black pepper. Garnish with lettuce or celery tops.

Potato Salad, Prince. Cut a quart of cold boiled potatoes fine and mince one quarter as much pickled cauliflower or cucumbers. Heat to the boiling point but do not cook long, one ounce of butter, one teaspoonful of made mustard, one tablespoonful made mustard, one tablespoonful of celery salt and four of vinegar. Pour hot over the potatoes and pickle. Toss lightly and serve when very cold.

Potato Salad with Mushrooms. Slice cold boiled potatoes in a dish and cover with fresh mushrooms, stewed and minced, using also the liquor in which they are stewed. The liquid from minced pickles, chow-chow, or sweet pickles may be used if preferred to the mushrooms. The potatoes will be greatly improved by dropping a little oil on each piece and letting it be absorbed before putting on the other seasoning. Let it stand in a cold place before serving.

Potato Salad with Egg. To a pint of chopped or sliced potatoes add half a cup of chopped cabbage and celery, a little minced pickle and parsley and a hard boiled egg. Serve with boiled dressing.

Potato Salad and Beets. Slice cold boiled potatoes in a bowl sprinkling each one with Worcestershire sauce and the red vinegar that has been on boiled beets, in equal quantities, to which a little onion juice has been added. Let it stand for some time in a cold place before serving. Garnish with pickled red beets, or mix the beets with the salad.

Hot Potato Salad. Cut enough breakfast bacon into small bits to fill a teacup, fry a light brown and remove: stir into the fat three tablespoonfuls of vinegar and pour over six or seven large potatoes that have been sliced and mixed with three large onions minced fine, all hot. Eat while hot.

Potato Salad with Herbs. Slice cold boiled potatoes and sprinkle with salt and a little oil. Then pour over them enough claret or other acid red wine to moisten them. Then mix with chopped endive or lettuce and sprinkle well with chervil and add tarragon or any other herb that is liked.

Potato Salad with Peppers and Olives. Arrange cold boiled potatoes in a flat dish into slices or cubes. Over them place a layer of shredded sweet peppers and another layer of olives. Serve with French dressing.

Potato Salad a la Ohio. Cut cold boiled potatoes into even slices and sprinkle with chopped parsley and tender onion in small quantities minced very fine. Salt to suit the taste. Make a dressing with two-thirds of a teacupful of medium strength vinegar, two whole eggs well beaten, one and a half tablespoonfuls of sugar, half a saltspoonful of Cayenne pepper, a saltspoonful of salt and one-third cupful of butter. Put the dressing on to cook in a boiler or bowl in hot water; when it boils or thickens take from the fire and, when cold, stir in one cup of cream. Then add all to the potato. It is well to prepare the dressing first and have it ready.

Macedoine Salads. This name is given to nearly all mixtures of cold boiled vegetables which, naturally, are of all degrees of merit. It is a common way of utilizing cold boiled vegetables that have been left over from a meal.

The effort is often regarded as a great success but a really good salad cannot be made of vegetables that are boiled together. The charm of these salads consists of the different flavors being kept quite distinct. They can be arranged in a most inviting manner, the different colored vegetables in rings or sections, and garnished with green leaves or flowers, the dressing being placed in the centre or poured around the edge, the whole to be lightly mixed together just before serving. Sometimes the different vegetables are all cut in the same shape, variety being given by color alone. The shapes may, however, be varied if desired, cubes, strips, slices, triangles and balls all being easily made and fancy shapes formed with any vegetable cutter. These mixed salads are acceptable when salad greens are difficult to get and have the advantage of being prepared and kept on ice for some time before wanted. Nearly every vegetable that can be boiled and retain its shape can be utilized in these salads: green peas, string and flageolet beans, cauliflower, beets, carrots, turnips, potatoes, celery roots, asparagus being among the number. The vegetables are quickly boiled if cut into small pieces before cooking but it injures the color and flavor of many of them. When time permits it is better to cook them whole and cut after they are cold. When new beets and young carrots are in season these salads are at their best.

Number 1. Boil separately in salted water beets, yellow and white turnips and carrots. Arrange in a dish according to fancy, sprinkle with chopped pickle, garnish with hard boiled eggs and serve with a French dressing.

Number 2. Take cold boiled vegetables, cutting the large ones in small pieces. If not already salt enough sprinkle a little salt over them. Arrange lettuce leaves like cups and place a portion of the prepared vegetables in the centre. Cover with mayonnaise dressing and serve.

Number 3. Have young carrots, new beets, new potatoes and young turnips boiled in separate salted waters. Have twice as much beet as any other vegetable, sprinkle them liberally with good vinegar. If the carrots are not naturally sweet, a little sugar or boiling in sweetened water will improve them. The turnips require more salt than the other vegetables. Arrange attractively on a flat dish keeping each vegetable separate. Garnish with whole boiled or shredded string beans, pieces of cauliflower, Brussels sprouts, asparagus tips, green peas or any of the vegetables cut into fancy shapes. Keep very cold, toss together just before helping and serve with mayonnaise dressing.

Macedoine with Cream. Arrange the boiled and cut vegetables in the centre of a suitable dish and sprinkle with tarragon or any vinegar preferred. Just before sending to table pour a border of rich cream around the vegetables and mix all together before helping. Green peas, new beets, potatoes, beans etc., are better with cream than cabbage and cauliflower.

Bean Salad. Cold boiled or baked beans will usually be found acceptable served with any good salad dressing. They can be mixed with cold potatoes and onions. The common white beans are liked served with a dressing made of salt, pepper, a tablespoonful of oil, one of French mustard and two of thick cream. Chopped pickles or small ones whole are a good garnish for beans.

Stuffed Beet Salad. Stuffed beets are prepared like tomato baskets. Boil fresh red beets until tender, take off the skin while hot, cut off the tops and scoop out the inside taking care not to break the outer walls. Cut a small piece off the bottom so they will stand upright and when very cold fill with any of the following mixtures, or any good salad mixture. Chopped celery mixed with mayonnaise. Cucumber salad, French dressing. Asparagus tips, French dressing. Soak the beets in water and fill with potato salad.

Select beets of uniform size to serve at one time, not too large, and place each on a leaf of lettuce.

Cauliflower Salad. When cauliflower is properly prepared it makes one of the best of salads but if coarse or tough is unfit to eat. Take a head of cauliflower white and fresh from the garden and soak for an hour in salt and water, to which some vinegar has been added, to remove any insects that may be hidden in it. Then, head downward, boil slowly and carefully until tender but do not boil to pieces. Put a little salt in the water with sliced onions if it is to be served with mayonnaise. If the white head can be kept whole and stood in a dish surrounded by lettuce leaves it will make a most attractive dish. If the cauliflower is tender and fresh it can easily be helped with a sharp spoon, a portion of the curd-like head being put upon each plate and passed with French dressing or sauce tartare. If mayonnaise is used it is well to sprinkle it with vinegar or lemon juice and let it stand awhile. When the head is broken up it can be arranged in a pile in the centre of the dish and surrounded by a border of cold boiled vegetables, sliced or trimmed into fancy shapes, beets, carrots, rings of okra, string beans etc., being used. The dressing is then poured over it and it is then sprinkled with mixed fine herbs, chervil, tarragon, mint or any other preferred.

Broccoli Salad. This plant is so like the cauliflower that it is best served in the same way. Bacon dressing is liked with it by some.

Beet Salads. Boiled or baked beet-root is used in combination with nearly every other vegetable in the formation of salads. When used as a garnish or in winter salads it is customary to pickle the slices by letting them stand in vinegar, but the delicate flavor of young sweets beets is injured by much vinegar. Chopped coriander leaves harmonize in flavor.

Number 1. Take six fair sized beets and bake in a slow oven until tender: when cold peel and cut into pieces of equal size, mix with five or six onions that have been cut into rounds and had boiling water poured over them twice. French or mayonnaise dressing.

Number 2. Take one-third boiled celerica and two-thirds baked or boiled beets cut into slices, with a few chicory leaves, blanched dandelions, or any chopped herb desired. French dressing.

Number 3. Arrange in the centre of a flat dish a little pile of boiled new potatoes cut into cubes and sprinkled with salt. Around them place a border of cold boiled small new beets cut into slices or quartered, then surround these with a border of pepper grass, cress, lettuce sprinkled with chopped nasturtium buds or tender leaves, and serve with Remoulade or some mild dressing.

Salad of Brussels Sprouts. Have as many fresh un-wilted Brussels sprouts as are wanted, soak and wash carefully in salted water and vinegar to remove dirt and insects. Boil briskly fifteen or twenty minutes, or until tender, in salted water in which a pinch of soda has been dissolved to keep them green. Drain, cool and serve with French dressing. The water in which they are boiled may have sliced onions, celery tops, thyme or any other herb desired used to give a slight flavor to the sprouts. Green peas or any cold boiled vegetables may be used for garnishing.

Okra Salad. Choose young fresh pods of okra and boil in salted water fifteen or twenty minutes or until they are tender but not until soft. Drain and put on ice and serve like asparagus, when cold, with French, vinaigrette or mayonnaise dressing. A pinch of cooking soda in the water will help their color and a bunch of sweet marjoram, thyme, basil, onion or any herb preferred may be boiled with them to impart a slight flavor. If wanted to mix with vegetable salads the pods can be cut in rings before boiling making an attractive garnish.

Marechal Salad. Boil two large solid heads of lettuce in salted water until tender. Then cut into eight pieces longitudinally, drain and cool. When cold put a spoonful of French dressing over each piece and sprinkle plentifully with boiled vegetables, potatoes, string beans etc., also mixed pickled onions, gherkins etc., covering the tops quite plentifully. Finish with some little balls or cubes of bread, toasted or baked brown bread, and cover with olive oil. Garnish with hard boiled eggs and a few leaves of green herbs.

Salad of Hop Sprouts. The young sprouts of green hops are considered excellent by those who have tried them. Wash carefully to remove insects, tie in bunches like asparagus and boil in salted water ten or twelve minutes. Drop in ice water to cool and harden them. Serve like asparagus with French dressing and vinaigrette sauce.

Maxixe Salad. This is a little cucumber-like vegetable from South America. Peel off the rough skin and cut in thin slices as you would a cucumber and dress with French dressing made with onion juice, or mix thinly sliced onion with it.

Martynia Salads. The pods of the martynia or martenoe are more commonly used for pickles but are enjoyed in salads by many people. Rub off the downy coating of very young tender pods, cut in slices and let stand in salt and vinegar for an hour or two, then drain and use for garnishing or mix in any green salad.

Fruit Salads.

—

SALADS in which fruits form a prominent part are becoming very popular. They are often served as a first course at luncheons or in place of a course of fruit at dessert. For a first course they should be rather acid or made with fruit of an acid nature, while later during a meal they are more enjoyed if sweetened and more highly flavored.

As a rule they are most attractive looking compounds often highly fragrant and appeal to all our senses. Almost any kind of acid fruit is nice to serve in this way. For eating with meats or birds the ordinary French dressing, omitting the onion, is good. For dessert, or at one of our American " Teas, " the cold sweet fruit mixtures are preferred. Neufchatel cheese is enjoyed with them at a late breakfast or luncheon. The fruit salads may be put into an ice cream freezer and cooled with the usual mixture of salt and ice.

When handsome glass or porcelain dishes, with silver ones to place them in, are not available a pretty way to serve fruit salads is in dainty glasses. Peaches, fresh figs and the many varieties of berries have always been popular with sugar and cream but, for variety, try one of the following methods which may be considerably varied by changing the fruits and proportions as the supplies change or the taste varies.

Mixed Fruit Salad. Fill delicate cups or glasses with fresh pine-apple, bananas and white grapes cut, halved and seeded, the pulp and juice of oranges and candied cherries, all the fruit to be cut rather fine. Cover them with a dressing made with four tablespoonfuls of powdered sugar, one gill of sherry, one tablespoonful maraschino and two of champagne. Stir until the sugar is dissolved and then pour over the fruit and let the glasses stand in a cold refrigerator an hour before serving. Another dressing is made with four tablespoonfuls of sugar and half a teaspoonful of cinnamon mixed with two tablespoonfuls of sherry and the same of Maderia. Some people delight in a mixture of acid fruit, currants, raspberries, morello cherries, strawberries etc., with candied fruit cut into small strips, angelica, citron, cherries, oranges and all the many kinds that are now prepared. Give a dressing of sugar and wine.

Mixed Fruit Salad No. 2. These salads are greatly admired by some people as table ornaments. They look best arranged on a large flat dish. Select a pineapple having a pretty top and carefully peel and slice so that the slices can be arranged in the centre of the dish in the original shape of the fruit. Sprinkle each slice with sugar and fasten the top of the pineapple in place with a wooden skewer if necessary. Peel and divide four or five oranges into sections, remove the seeds and arrange the sections about the pineapple. Peel four large bananas, cut into slices lengthwise and arrange them in regular order about the sides of the dish like the spokes of a wheel. Fill the space between with any attractive fruit obtainable such as strawberries, raspberries or pomegranite grains. Dust powdered sugar over them just before being served and help with more sugar and cream or, to half a pint of clear sugar syrup add a glass of good brandy, or two of sherry wine, and pour over the fruit.

Fruit Salad with Jelly. Make a rich sweet lemon or wine jelly in accordance with any recipe that is liked, having it rather stiff as the juice of the fruit tends to thin it Surround the jelly mould with ice. Put in a layer of jelly and let it get firm, then a layer of ripe fruit of any kind that is tender yet firm such as raspberries, apricots, peaches, bananas, oranges or plums. Cover this layer of fruit with

jelly and let harden again and continue this until the mould
is full. Keep on ice until wanted. Sweet cream may be
served with it. A clear transparent jelly with the prettily
arranged fruit inside of it makes a most effective dish.

French Fruit Salad. Keep the fruit in a cold place until
ready to prepare and then take grapes with the seeds ex-
tracted and skins taken off, strawberries, raspberries, sliced
bananas, oranges and pineapples in about equal proportions.
Dress with champagne and sugar and serve freezing cold.
Use a silver bowl filled with cracked ice with a glass bowl
inside into which the salad is heaped. This salad is enjoyable both in hot and cold weather.

French Fruit Salad No. 2. This is a combination fruit
salad that can be made in winter when the fruits named are
in the market. Blanch the meat of a dozen English walnuts.
With a very sharp knife skin and seed about two dozen
white grapes. Slice three bananas and divide two large
oranges into lobes cutting each lobe into three pieces. Arrange some of each on a few leaves of lettuce or separate
plates, or mix altogether on a pretty dish and serve with
mayonnaise dressing as cold as possible.

Grape Fruit and Lettuce. A delicious and unique salad
is made by cutting grape fruit or shaddock in halves and,
with a spoon, taking out all the pulp being careful to preserve the juice. Put in a salad bowl with fresh crisp lettuce
leaves, allowing one medium size head of lettuce for each
grape fruit. When ready to serve mix with a dressing
made with the juice. Have the juice cold and drop in oil
while stirring vigorously. Three of oil to one spoonful of
juice is about the right proportion although the proportions
vary according to the conditions of the ingredients. To
every three tablespoonfuls of this mixture allow half a tea-
spoon of salt and a quarter teaspoonful of pepper. Stir until emulsion is formed, pour over the salad, toss lightly
about and serve at once. The spoon may be rubbed with

garlic or a few drops of onion juice may be added to the salad if desired. Be most careful that no small pieces of tne white skin of the grape fruit find their way into the bowl or the salad will be bitter and disagreeable.

Grape Fruit with Mayonnaise. Peel a grape fruit and divide in sections: split the membrane and carefully extract the pulp dividing into little natural sections that will hold the juice, breaking them as little as possible. Put the tender leaves of two small heads or one large head of lettuce in a salad bowl and mingle with the prepared grape fruit; gave a sprinkle of salt and set in a cold place. When ready to serve, cover with mayonnaise dressing, mixing all well together just before helping.

Cherry Salad No. 1. Remove the stones from a dish of fine black cherries, sprinkle well with powdered sugar and add a wineglassful each of Curacoa and sherry wine to a quart of fruit. Mix well and cool on ice before sending to table.

Cherry Salad No. 2. Stone a pound of large acid cherries saving the juice. Peel and cut into thin slices a cucumber of medium size. Blanch and chop fine a dozen sweet almonds. Mix all these in a salad bowl or fancy dish with the white parts of two heads of lettuce and pour over them eight tablespoonfuls of powdered sugar, two tablespoonfuls of lemon juice, two gills of sherry and two tablespoonfuls of maraschino. Stir all together until the sugar is dissolved. Keep as cool as possible until served.

Cherry Salad No. 3. Remove the stones from half a pound of ripe but firm cherries. Shell as many hazel nuts as you have cherries, remove as much of the brown skin covering the kernel as possible, and place one nut in the centre of each cherry in place of the stone. Arrange on lettuce leaves or in the centre of the bowl with lettuce about them, and dress with plain mayonnaise made with a little lemon juice in place of all or part of the vinegar, but do not have it too acid.

Cherry Salad No. 4. Cherries in aspic jelly either with or without nuts are regarded with much favor by some people. An attractive way is to have a border of the jelly and when ready to serve fill the centre with cherries and shredded celery in equal quantities, mixed with mayonnaise. Some of the aspic jelly whipped until frothy and mixed with them, laid on top, will be attractive.

Pear Salad. Peel and slice, or divide into sections lengthwise, five sweet summer pears that are ripe but not soft. Sprinkle fine sugar over them with a little maraschino, or ginger syrup may be used both to sweeten and flavor. Serve with a little cream.

Acid Pear Salad. Acid pears, not too ripe, made into a salad are especially nice served with any water fowl. Peel the fruit and cut into thin slices being careful to remove the core and any hard or imperfect parts. Serve immediately with about an equal quantity of lettuce. A mayonnaise dressing is usually preferred with it but a French dressing is good used with or without onions.

Alligator Pear Salad. The Avocado or aguacata which has been given the senseless name of alligator pear by English speaking people, is the fruit of a tree (*Persea gratisssima*) native of tropical America. It is the favorite fruit for salads of those accustomed to its use and as the cultivation of the tree extends in the Gulf states, and the fruit finds its way more freely to the northern markets, its popularity increases.

The taste for this pear, like that for tomatoes, is an acquired one. Like most other salads this is preferred by Americans with a simple dressing. Cut the pear shaped fruit lengthwise and remove the large hard yellow seeds. Then sprinkle over each half, salt, pepper, vinegar or lemon juice and eat the inside with a spoon. An abundance of fruit must be had for this way of serving, so when the fruit is scarce or expensive it had better be peeled and cut into long thin strips and served with a French dressing to which a few drops of onion juice are a great improvement. Like all fruit salads it should be as cold as possible when served.

Mexican Alligator Pear Salad. This is called the Queen of Salads. Six alligator pears and six tomatoes peeled and sliced. One rareripe sliced very thin, and half a cupful of fresh coriander leaves. Salt, oil and vinegar as in a French dressing.

Prickly Pear Salad. The Indian fig or prickly pear in all its varieties can be made into most inviting salads. Stick a fork into the fruit and with a sharp knife cut off the skin. Avoid handling the fruit before peeling as there are often small spines left on the pears that will prove extremely annoying. Cut the fruit into small slices and mix with lettuce and mayonnaise dressing. If the fruit is of a large Southern variety it can be peeled and sliced into a dish sprinkled with sugar with the juice of an orange or lemon and a wineglassful of brandy added.

Orange Salad Number 1. Peel and divide into lobes, removing all particles of white skin and the seeds, serve on lettuce leaves with mayonnaise dressing. This is rather a heavy salad but is good to serve with venison or other game. Large acid oranges are best to use.

Orange Salad Number 2. Remove seeds and skin and divide the oranges into lobes arranged neatly on a dish. Dust powdered sugar over them and flavor with a little Chartreuse, maraschino and brandy or rum: put on ice and when cold and ready to serve moisten with five or six pieces of loaf sugar with the spirit, arrange on top of the oranges, set on fire and send it to table burning.

Orange Salad Number 3. Arrange a border of cold boiled rice around a dish and fill the centre with peeled and sliced oranges with sugar sprinkled over all. Cool on ice and when ready to serve pour over the top one or two wineglassfuls of arrack.

Orange Salad Number 4. Make this salad in the proportions of one good apple to two oranges all pared and sliced and arranged in layers, lightly sprinkled with fresh powdered cinnamon, a glass of sherry poured over the top and a heaping tablespoonful, more if the fruit is very acid, of sugar sprinkled over the fruit.

Orange Salad Number 5. This is the old fashioned mixture which probably first came into use soon after the discovery of America. Arrange on a dish alternate layers of peeled and sliced oranges, with grated or dessicated cocoanut sprinkled with fine white sugar. Sliced pineapple is often mixed with it and it can be flavored with a little sherry or other light wines.

Orange Salad Number 6. Peel and cut sour oranges in thick slices, or, if sweet oranges must be used, squeeze a little lemon juice over each slice, and remove the seeds. Make a dressing in the proportion of three tablespoonfuls of oil to one of lemon juice, salt, paprika or Cayenne pepper. Serve with game.

Orange Salad Number 7. Carefully remove both the yellow and white skins from the oranges and separate into natural segments. Place five or six of these on each plate and cover with the following dressing. Two eggs, one teaspoonful mustard, two tablespoonfuls of sugar, one teaspoonful of cornstarch, one tablespoonful of butter, one-half teaspoonful of pepper. Beat the eggs a little but not until light: stir in sugar, then butter, mustard and pepper. Dissolve the cornstarch in a little of the vinegar. Next pour vinegar over eggs etc. Place the bowl in a boiler or basin of hot water and stir the dressing until it thickens like soft custard. When hot stir in cornstarch. When cold stir in salt and a little cream. This dressing will keep for a long time before salt and cream are added.

Orange Salad Number 8. This salad should be served with game or rich roasts. Peel the oranges and remove all the white skin, slice them very thin. Arrange the slices on a flat dish and sprinkle walnut meat and leaves of water cress thickly over them repeating the layers as often as wished. Put a border of cress around the dish. Have a remoulade dressing, or make a dressing with lemon or sour orange juice, two tablespoonfuls of juice to four of oil, salt and a little Cayenne pepper. Acid oranges are best for this salad.

Green Apple Salad. Take six Rhode Island Greening apples and two heads of celery, all cut fine and served at once with mayonnaise dressing.

Apple Salad. Salads of apples are excellent with cold roast meats in winter. Have everything cold and do not cut the apples until ready to serve. Chop or shred very fine one good sized Spanish or sweet pepper, carefully removing all seeds and the core. Break a head of lettuce into a salad bowl and slice over it six crisp, tart, highly flavored apples. Long narrow slices are most attractive. Sprinkle the chopped peppers evenly among the apples. Dress with two tablespoonfuls of lemon juice, six of oil and a saltspoonful of salt. Mix well, pour over the salad, stir lightly and serve.

Apple and Walnut Salad is made the same as the preceding using the meat of English walnuts that have been scalded in hot water and the dark skin removed, instead of the shredded pepper. About a cupful of walnut meats will be required. Mayonnaise dressing is liked with this.

Apple and Celery Salad is good with game. Have equal quantities of finely sliced very cold apples and celery, sprinkled with salt and mix lightly together. Cover with mayonnaise dressing, or, if preferred, use French dressing. Some epicures hold that mayonnaise should never be served with roast meats.

Raspberry Salads. Ripe fresh cold raspberries are so delicious when in perfection that any addition excepting a little sugar seems an injury, but a variety in the service is sometimes desirable.

For a quart of ripe raspberries squeeze out the juice of half a pint of currants, add half a teaspoonful of freshly ground cinnamon and half a wineglass of brandy. Sweeten to taste and pour over the cold fruit. Another way is to arrange the raspberries neatly in a dish sprinkling powdered sugar them. Squeeze out the juice of a fine orange, mix with a wineglassful of maraschino and pour over the berries. Still another way is to arrange a centre of white currants, white raspberries or any different colored fruit from the berries, and then place a border of red raspberries around them. A round rather flat dish with a raised edge is best. By making a cylinder of a strip of paper about as stiff as writing paper, and filled with the white fruit, putting the red outside the paper and carefully pulling the paper up when all is ready, the arrangement is easily made. Whip a wineglassful of sherry wine into a pint of cream and serve with the fruit and fine sugar. Brandy or some *liqueur* can be used instead of sherry.

Strawberry Salad. The true admirers of the strawberry do not want the natural flavor of the fruit destroyed by too many additions, but some people are unable to eat them plain and such will find them harmless used in the following ways.

Make a pint of good claret wine quite sweet with white sugar and add to it a small glassful of Curacoa and pour over the fruit. Chartreuse or maraschino may be used instead of Curacoa.

Squeeze the juice from two oranges and mix with it a wineglassful of brandy and one of water and pour over a quart of fruit that has been sprinkled with sugar.

Make a syrup of half a pound of white sugar dissolved in enough water to make a thin syrup: add a wineglassful of brandy and one of Chatreuse or Curacoa and about half a teaspoonful of grated nutmeg. Serve separately putting a little over each portion of fruit before eating.

Quince Salad. A salad that is relished with fish and game, and that is a pleasing novelty to most people, can be made by paring and slicing a few ripe quinces and dressing with French dressing. Any minced herbs, tarragon, spearmint, chives, marjoram etc., can be minced and sprinkled over them or flavored vinegars may be used in the dressing.

Currant Salad. Currants can be dressed with any of the mixtures of sugar and wine suggested for use with other berries, cream and sugar. Mixed with a small quantity of mayonnaise dressing, made with mustard, and served on lettuce, they are good to accompany roast birds or game.

Fig Salad. This is considered by many an improvement over fresh figs and cream which delights all who are fond of figs. Quarter twenty-five fresh ripe figs into a pretty bowl or dish and pour over, as fast as you put them in, half a pint of clear strained honey; let them stand on ice. When ready to serve whip a small glass of brandy into a quart of rich cream and pour over the figs.

Mulberry Salad. This fruit is often difficult to serve but makes a wholesome highly flavored salad. Pick the fruit over and arrange in a bowl or dish sprinkling fine sugar plentifully all through it. To a quart of fruit allow one wineglassful of Chatreuse, the juice of one orange, one tablespoonful of ginger syrup (from pressed Canton ginger) or a little powdered ginger if without the syrup. Pour over the fruit and serve. Cream may be added at table.

Pineapple Salad. When pineapples are plentiful a pleasant variation to the plain fruit can be had by peeling carefully and slicing, or better still, tearing the fruit into shreds with a fork which makes it lighter, leaving out the core and hard parts. Sprinkle with fine sugar and for each fruit allow a tablespoonful of brandy and one of Curacoa with a small wineglassful of arrack. Mix with some of the juice and pour over the whole. Maraschino and brandy are sometimes used. Serve very cold.

Melon Salad. A really good melon should never be injured by the addition of anything else other than a little salt. Those that are more or less insipid in flavor may be improved if served with a French or mayonnaise dressing. Cut the melon in rather long thin strips and serve as cold as possible.

Fruit Salad. This is a good fruit salad to make in winter or when fresh fruit is not available. The quantity given is sufficient for eight persons. Eight oranges, one banana, one-half pound candied cherries, one-half can of peaches, one-half can pears and one-sixth can of pineapple. Cut all the fruit into "chunks" not slices. Carefully remove skin and all white pulp from the oranges and cut into chunks as well. Have a dressing of one-half cup of mayonnaise made with the yolks of two eggs only, and enough oil to complete the half-cupful. Just before the salad is wanted mix the mayonnaise with one and one-half pints of whipped cream, pour over the salad and gently mix just before serving. None of the juices of the fruits should enter the salad and if the oranges are very sour they should be sugared and then drained before using.

Nut Salads are growing in favor and nuts are better served as a flavoring by themselves, in a plain salad, than in rich meat or other salads where their distinctive flavor is lost. Pecans, English and American walnuts, chestnuts, butternuts, almonds and even peanuts may be used. The delicacy and appearance of all are improved by scalding in hot water and removing the brown skins. Chestnuts should be boiled fifteen or twenty minutes before the shells are taken off. Have nice tender lettuce, sprinkle it plentifully with the prepared nut meat and serve with a French dressing without onion. Celery can be used instead of lettuce and is often preferred with chestnuts.

When the chestnuts used are large they should be cut into pieces. The nuts are sometimes used mixed, although one kind at a time is to be preferred. An English walnut salad is made by soaking the meat of about two dozen English walnuts in lemon juice for two hours and then mixing them with water cress and a French dressing. Green English walnuts are sometimes sliced and mixed with salads. Apples, celery and nuts are combined by taking a cupful of shredded celery, cut apple and nut meats, mixing and pouring over all a teaspoonful of oil and a little less quantity of lemon juice. Let it stand before serving and then dress with mayonnaise.

Fancy Salads.

THE following are among the curiosities of salad making and are more popular abroad than in this country.

There is a large number of impracticable ones, too elaborate to eat, that are not given here. Most of the so-called high class salads in France are largely flavored with truffles. When ripe and fresh these are extremely delicate but as we get them in this country, dry and canned, they are devoid of flavor and a poor condiment.

Salad d' Estree. This is a very old recipe. Cut celery in fine strips and curl by soaking for a time in ice water: drain and mix with sliced truffles that have been stewed in wine. Oil, pepper, vinegar and salt was the old fashioned dressing, but mayonnaise is now used. Celery and chestnuts make a good imitation of the original salad.

Salade Rachel. This is made the same as the preceding using sliced celeriac instead of celery.

Salad a la Mirabeau. Cut boiled potatoes into slices or cubes and have as many small oysters and shrimp, half of each. Season plentifully with sliced truffles and French dressing.

California Salad. This is a salad in name only and is more appreciated by Bohemians than housekeepers. Wash as many fresh sweet oranges as may be wanted, in order to soften the skin and let the oil out. Slice at once, unpeeled, in a dish or punch bowl, slicing as thin as possible, sprinkling each layer with sugar and packing closely in the dish. Over all pour enough whiskey to cover well. After standing half an hour or more it can be served as a cordial in *liqueur* glasses and is regarded by many as delectable. Small crackers are good with it.

Long Salads. This name is given to an arrangement of
differently flavored, finely cut salads arranged on a plate so
the eater receives the sensation of the different flavors in
succession. Macedoine with different herb flavors can be
used.

Salade a la Jockey Club. Take a quart of cold boiled
asparagus tips, sprinkle with minced chervil and sliced
truffles and serve with French dressing.

Jardiniere Salad. This is made of cold cooked vegetables,
carrots, beets, turnips, potatoes, asparagus tips, beans, peas,
cauliflower, okra, arranged with lettuce leaves, cresses, chervil or other salad greens. With a little ingenuity the carrots
can be cut to resemble marigolds and the other vegetables
to resemble roses, narcissus and other flowers. When arranged with the greens in a basket-shaped dish a pretty re-
semblance to a basket of flowers can be made. Use any
dressing liked.

Bird's Nest Salad. Make as many eggs as are wanted
by taking cream, plain cottage or pot cheese and rubbing a
little green coloring matter or spinach juice into it, to color
it a light green. A pink tint can be given with a little
beet or berry juice and a yellowish one by using yolk of
egg. Let some of the manufactured eggs remain pure white.
They can be speckled to look like bird eggs with coarse
red or black pepper. For those who do not like cheese,
eggs can be made of the yolks of hard boiled eggs moistened with cream. Mould the eggs with the smooth side of
a butter pat or wooden knife into egg shaped balls about
the size of a robbin's or pigeon's egg, and arrange from
three to five in nests made of shredded lettuce on the centre leaves of head lettuce arranged like a cup, and trimmed
to look like a bird's nest. These nests can be placed on a
flat dish or on individual plates. Serve with cream, mayonnaise or French dressing. Cheese straws are good to
serve with these salads.

Grand Salad. Jane Cromwell's grand salad was an old fashioned elaboration composed of equal parts of boiled shrimp, boiled turnips cut up, almonds, raisins, capers and pickles mixed and spiced, and dressed with a little sugar and what would correspond to a plain dressing in these days.

Cardinal Salad. Flake up half a pound of white meat of a cold boiled fish and cover with vinegar that beets have been pickled in. Cut up an equal quantity of young fresh boiled beets. Arrange the leaves of a red cabbage on a dish (some of the cabbage can be chopped and mixed with the salad if liked.) Mix the fish and beet and place on the cabbage leaves and dress with a French dressing made with a few drops of tobasco sauce or red pepper. Decorate with hard boiled eggs cut in slices.

Violet Salad. For a violet lunch or dinner a salad can be made of the blue violet so common in May throughout the northern states. Have them freshly gathered, pick from the stems and mix with a small quantity of mayonnaise. Keep a handful of the largest blossoms to scatter over the top and serve at once: or, sprinkly lightly with salt and dress with lemon juice and sugar. Candied angelica stalks can be shredded and added to the flowers.

Salade de Saisons is a name that has given rise to some confusion. It means no particular salad, but any one that is in season.

Colored Salads. As colored lunches and dinners, so called, are admired by many it may be well to suggest a few appropriate salads. For a Crimson dinner a salad of beets naturally suggest itself. Some tomatoes are also crimson in color and the so-called red cabbages. White vegetables may be colored with beet juice as can also the dressing. Crimson fruit may be used such as blood oranges, blood peaches and the "Sops of Wine" apple which is red all through, berries etc. Crimson flowers can of course be used to decorate the dish that holds the salad bowl.

"**Green**" **Salads** suggest themselves so naturally that they need not be specified. Spinach green may be used to color the dressing.

"**White**" **Salads** can be made of potatoes, white turnips, the heart of celery, chicken, white fish, stalks of lettuce leaves and many other things that will suggest themselves. Use white wine or other colorless vinegar and the whites only when eggs are used.

"**Pink**" **Salads** are numerous. Shrimp or prawn, salmon, pink trout, pink celery, beets, radishes and any pink flowers may be used. The coral of lobster will color the dressing, or some prepared coloring matter may be used.

"**Orange**" **Colored Salads** can be made from carrots, young squashes, cantaloupes etc. The yolk of egg can be used liberally omitting the white. Orange colored flowers, nasturtiums, buttercups etc., and even sunflower petals, lantana etc., are sometimes used.

"**Yellow**" **Salads** are made of yellow tomatoes, sweet potatoes, the yellow part of carrots and young squashes.

Green and White Salad. For a green and white luncheon a pretty salad is made by taking small Bermuda or other white turnips of uniform size and; after peeling, boil in salted water about half an hour or until they are tender but not soft, and then scoop the centre out with a round knife making shallow cups. Fill these with cold boiled French or green peas mixed with mayonnaise dressing, and place on leaves of lettuce.

Red Vegetable Salad. Take about one pint of cold boiled red beets, cut rather fine, and about as much cold boiled potato. Salt the potatoes and dress liberally with the red vinegar in which beets have been pickled. Celery may be used in place of the potato if desired. Shred about one pint of red cabbage and sprinkle with salt and six tablespoonfuls of oil. Mix all these together and let stand in a cold place long enough to be chilled thoroughly before serving. French dressing made with onion juice can be added at table just before serving.

Bouquet Salad.   Take four hard boiled eggs and chop fine, one good sized head of lettuce or two smaller ones, about a pint of water cress or pepper grass leaves, or the tender leaves and buds of nasturtium and more of the flowers.   Have a bunch of nasturtium flowers and buttercups. Examine the flowers carefully and see that no insects are concealed in them. A few rose petals of which pink and white are the most attractive can be added, as well as the flowers of horseradish, cabbage, turnip or any of the cress family being careful to use only a little of the strong kinds. Petals of fruit blossoms of any kind may be added in small quantities. Mince up the nasturtium leaves, if you use them, but let the flower petals be fresh and unbroken. Use French dressing made without onion but with a little sugar added. Arrange a layer of lettuce and cress in the bottom of the bowl, sprinkle with egg and dressing and then a few of the flowers: repeat this until the desired quantity is secured having more of the flowers in the top layer with some of the more attractive leaves nicely arranged. The petals of peach blossoms give a delicate flavor of bitter almonds and are good in fruit salads generally.

French Snail Salad. Select the largest sized snails to be had. Wash in salted water and boil until they can be taken from the shells easily, say fifteen to twenty-five minutes. Pick from the shells and while still hot pour over them a French dressing made with tartare vinegar, or, if common vinegar is used, add a few drops of onion juice. Let them cool and stand at least an hour. When ready to serve they can be eaten with plain bread and butter or mixed with lettuce in a salad bowl with more French dressing, mayonnaise or remoulade sauce. Common garden snails are good eating.

Miscellaneous Salads.

MANY of the following salads may properly be termed "national" being the favorite salads of the people in the several countries the name of which is given the salad. Some of them will be found well suited to American tastes, while others will come under the heading of articles for which an acquired taste must be gained by repeated eating.

German Salad. Mince fine one onion, two cucumbers, one pickled pepper, two ounces shredded red pickled cabbage, one sliced beet, two heads bleached endive, two large boiled potatoes sliced, two hard boiled eggs, half a dozen large sorrel leaves and a dozen tarragon leaves. Dress with half a pint of Rhine wine, six tablespoonfuls of oil and two of tarragon vinegar. Mix all with a pound of fresh beef, boiled or roasted, cut into narrow slices, and place in an ice box for four hours before serving.

German Salad with Sausage. Boil four Frankfort sausages twenty minutes and cut into half inch pieces. Throw half a pound of sauerkraut into boiling water and let it remain ten minutes: drain, cool and mix in a salad bowl with the sausage. Cut up two black radishes and arrange around the salad, sprinkling it with minced shallot, pickles and capers. Set the dish in the ice box for some hours before serving and dress with French dressing.

Ferguson Quick Salad. Two heads of celery sliced, a can of French peas, one can small French beans, one-half pound "Deerfield" sausage fried brown and cut into dice shaped pieces. Rub the bowl with a raw onion before putting in the salad. Mayonnaise dressing.

Russian Salads. Just now it is the fashion to attribute many elaborate compounds to our Russian friends and some of them would doubtless make a Muscovite shudder, for they remind us of the cook who puts into his salads anything and everything handy. Those here given have been highly recommended but some of them would be more relished by a skating party than for a mid-summer breakfast.

Russian Summer Salad. Put in a salad bowl two torn leaves of lettuce, one of endive, a sliced tomato, half a peeled and sliced cucumber, and a chopped beet with a tea-spoonful of capers. Make a dressing with the yolks of two hard boiled eggs, half a teaspoonful of salt and half as much pepper, one of fine sugar, two tablespoonfuls of oil, one of white vinegar and one gill of cream. Pour over the salad and sprinkle the chopped white of the boiled egg on top.

Russian Meat Salad. Cut into pieces of equal size cold fowl, roast beef, boiled ham, beef tongue, lean mutton or any other meat on hand. Arrange each kind separately keeping them apart by placing boned anchovies between. Keep the centre open by placing an inverted cup on the plate or dish. Make a thick border of shredded lettuce or scatter the lettuce over the top. Remove the cup and fill the centre with tartare sauce. Just before serving mix all together.

Russian Tomato and Sardine Salad. Arrange a bed of torn lettuce in a salad bowl. Peel four tomatoes of medium size, cut fine and mix with six sardines chopped up after the skin and bones have been removed. Place on the lettuce and serve either with mayonnaise or French dressing.

Russian Mixed Salad. Take about two ounces each of chopped roast chicken, beef, ham, tongue and mutton, two heads of lettuce and three of celery cut fine, four truffles and twelve anchovies. Mix carefully with eight tablespoonfuls of tartare sauce and serve.

Russian Salad of all Seasons. Take two each of boiled red beets and potatoes cut in small pieces, two red onions sliced thin, two heads of celery cut small, a head of chicory or any fresh salad plant that is in season. A teaspoonful of capers and pickled nasturtium seeds, six large olives cut in thin slices. Put all in a salad bowl and pour over a dressing made with the yolk of one raw egg and three hard boiled ones, cutting the latter into ringlets and saving the white portions, six to eight tablespoonfuls of oil, two of tartare vinegar, a teaspoonful of made mustard, half a teaspoonful of white pepper and one teaspoonful of salt with a sprinkling of Cayenne pepper. Pour over the salad then sprinkle over the top two heaping tablespoonfuls of cavaire. Garnish with the egg ringlets having round pieces of red beet cut and fitted into the centres of the yolk to represent rubies. Use lettuce or some green herb for a border to the dish.

Russian Aspic Salad. Fill the outside of a double mould with a clear aspic jelly. This can be more or less elaborately decorated by using pieces of colored vegetables cut into the semblance of leaves or flowers. Capers or olives are fastened into place with a little jelly before the mould is filled, or the jelly may be left clear as preferred. Mix the vegetable macedoine which is to go in the centre with a mayonnaise made with jelly instead of eggs, and cover the whole with jelly. When wanted turn out on a flat dish and garnish with lettuce, parsley or some green herb.

Individual Russian Aspic Salads. Ornament the bottom of a cup or small mould with boiled carrot, green peas, capers etc., fashioned in any form fancied; fix them with a little clear aspic jelly and when hard fill the moulds with jelly. When all has hardened scoop the middle carefully out of the jelly with a hot spoon and fill with macedoine or vegetables or meat salad made with thick jelly mayonnaise and finish with clear mayonnaise. Serve on cress or lettuce with mayonnaise dressing.

Suedoise Salad. Peel and slice two cold boiled potatoes, one small beet, one half a carrot, and one uncooked sour apple. Mix in the salad bowl with the meat picked from a boned herring, cut small, and two ounces of chopped cold boiled beef tongue. Sprinkle with salt and pepper and dress with a teaspoonful of vinegar and one and a half table-spoonfuls of oil. Scatter chopped parsley over the top.

Sweet Potato Salad. Cut boiled sweet potatoes into cubes or squares of convenient size and mix with an equal amount of celery cut small and dress with French dressing. Garnish with sliced olives and parsley.

Dutch Salad. Pick the meat from one salt herring and mince into small pieces. Mix with half a pint of smoked ham and sausage cut into dice and the same quantity of cold roast fowl or veal. Also cut into dice the same quantity of boiled beet, cucumber pickle and a pint of cold boiled potatoes cut a little larger. Dress with three tablespoonfuls of tarragon vinegar, eight of oil, one of mixed French mustard with pepper and salt to suit the taste. Mix these well together and sprinkle with chopped yolks and whites of hard boiled eggs, capers and stoned olives. Ornament still more with washed, split and boned anchovies.

Cuban Salad. Break up four dry and brittle soda crackers, shred two sweet Spanish peppers, carefully removing the core and seeds, slice as thinly as possible one large Spanish onion, skin and bone six anchovies, mince fine and mix all together. Lettuce may be added if desired. Dress liberally with French dressing.

Japanese Salad. Take three dozen mussels boil just long enough to make the shells open, remove from the shells, cut off the black heads and stew in a cup of white wine with a sliced onion for a few minutes only, being careful not to boil. Have an equal quantity of hot boiled potatoes and pour the wine from the mussels over them together with

salt, pepper and six tablespoonfuls of oil. When cold, mix
with the mussels adding a little vinegar or lemon juice if
the wine was not acid enough. Add also chopped parsley,
burnet, tarragon or any sweet herb liked. Serve a mild
boiled dressing or Hollandaise sauce with them. Very small
oysters or clams may be used in place of mussels.

Spanish Salad. Sprinkle a little salt over some white endive leaves and pile in the middle of a salad dish. Boil four
eggs hard, cut in quarters, put a shrimp or some chopped
lobster or crab meat with a little seasoning in place of the
yolks and stand the whites about the endive. Chop up the
yolks and strew about the endive. Peel and quarter four
tomatoes and stand the quarters between the whites of egg.
Shred very finely or chop small, the mild part of a sweet
pepper, leaving out the seeds and core, and scatter on top
of the egg yolk. When ready to help pour over all a
French dressing made with onion juice and mix together.

Italian Salad. Cut a carrot and a turnip of large size
into fancy strips with a vegetable cutter, or into cubes with
a knife and boil separately in salted water: ten minutes for
the carrot and fifteen for the turnip should be long enough.
When cold, pile in the centre of the dish and arrange
around them the breast of a chicken cut into strips and on
these clusters of sliced truffles, broiled mushrooms and asparagus tips, or brussels sprouts. Mix a tablespoonful of
anchovy sauce, half a teaspoonful of salt, a quarter tablespoonful each of vinegar and oil. Make a hole in the centre of the salad and pour in the dressing. Stop the hole
with a piece of cauliflower and just before serving mix all
together.

A Noutese Salad. Skin three or four mild flavored
onions and bake until tender cutting off the top and putting
a lump of butter on each one and seasoning with salt and
pepper. When cold remove any hard parts and cut in
quarters: mix with four hard boiled eggs and six sardines

chopped. Season with chervil, tarragon or parsley. Mix a teaspoonful of curry powder with mayonnaise or boiled dressing and serve with the salad.

Bread Salad is not popular in this country but in countries where everything goes into the salad bowl it forms a favorable way of utilizing broken pieces of bread. Bread salads are simply the addition to the vegetable salad of stale bread with the crust removed and cut into small pieces of even shape. They absorb the superfluous dressing. Sometimes before being put into the salad bowl the bread is dressed with oil. It is a wholesome food and children are exceedingly fond of it. Do not have enough bread to make the salad dry or enough dressing to make the bread sodden.

INDEX.

Lightning Source UK Ltd.
Milton Keynes UK
UKHW012249220422
401922UK00002B/452